MULTIMEDIA SECURITY PARADIGMS

A Peer-to-Peer Network Perspective

Dr. Ramesh Shahabadkar
Dr. S. Sai Satyanarayana Reddy

INDIA • SINGAPORE • MALAYSIA

Notion Press

Old No. 38, New No. 6
McNichols Road, Chetpet
Chennai - 600 031

First Published by Notion Press 2018
Copyright © Dr. Ramesh Shahabadkar & Dr. S. Sai Satyanarayana Reddy 2018
All Rights Reserved.

ISBN 978-1-64324-989-6

CONTENTS

CHAPTER 1

ESSENTIALS OF SECURITY ASPECTS IN PEER-TO-PEER NETWORK ENABLED MULTIMEDIA DATA TRANSMISSION

1.1 OVERVIEW

Peer-to-peer (P2P) communication enables an approach which performs content distribution over the internet in which digital files are transferred between peers or computers. It is usually used for content distribution and file sharing with the ease of transmission. There exist another model of a network called client-server model, where content is stored on the servers. In client-server models, when the client request for the content, it is delivered by the server that forms a one to many distribution systems. With P2P, the client machines are peers and communicate with one another. A computer in the network can submit a request for specific content, and any peer in the network that has a copy of the file can send it, resulting in a many-to-many model that does not rely on a central repository.

Because they do not rely on a central server to deliver content, P2P networks tend to be faster and much more reliable—as long as at least one other computer in the network has a file, others can access it. Any user of a P2P network is as likely to be a contributor as a consumer, and, in this sense, P2P approximates the original conception of the Internet as a network of connections among individuals and organizations that give and take information.

1.2 PEER-TO-PEER (P2P) NETWORKING CHARACTERISTICS

In Peer-to-Peer overlay networks, a distributed system interconnects a set of nodes which are well capable of sharing resources such as content, CPU cycles, storage and bandwidth, and also accommodating transient populations of nodes while maintaining acceptable connectivity and performance within a self-organized network topology. It also doesn't require intermediation or support of a global centralized server or authority [1]. P2P networks are virtual overlay networks built on an underlay network. That means each entity in the underlay network has a corresponding identity in the overlay networks. Different types have been defined as hierarchical P2P network and flat P2P network. Hierarchical P2P network [2] utilizes multiple levels of hierarchy to distribute the overlay node and it can also be classified into three categories: unstructured, structured and hybrid networks. However, the P2P networks still suffer from vulnerable network scenario as a result of the big variety of illegal contents that are distributed by those applications. As an example, for video streaming, major firms worry to possess their contents "pirated" and decentralized while not respecting the digital rights.

Many analysis works projected solutions for a P2P video delivery however don't extremely take into thought the legal aspects of it [3] [4] [5] [6]. Their power to accommodate massive amounts of users, beside their resilience to churn, responsibility, and low price are a number of the explanations why they're most well-liked over dedicated servers or content distribution solutions. In spite of those benefits, or even as a result of them, some P2P options create these systems harder to defend against some categories of attacks. Security-wise, P2P streaming systems are more difficult than alternative P2P applications as a result of they're a lot of liable to QoS fluctuations. The current paper will discuss about a novel security protocol and how it can be implemented on heavier multimedia applications on insecure P2P network. The system also discusses about the performance analysis with respect to the similar work carried out in past.

One possible classification of peer-to-peer networks is according to their degree of centralization:

1.2.1 Pure Peer-to-Peer

- Peers act as equals, merging the roles of clients and server
- There is no central server managing the network
- There is no central router

1.2.2 Hybrid Peer-to-Peer

- Has a central server that keeps information on peers and responds to requests for that information.
- Peers are responsible for hosting available resources (as the central server does not have them), for letting the central server know what resources they want to share, and for making its shareable resources available to peers that request it.
- Route terminals are used addresses, which are referenced by a set of indices to obtain an absolute address.

Some examples of pure peer-to-peer application layer networks designed for file sharing are Gnutella and Freenet. Meanwhile some may also categorize peer-to-peer networks into the following categories:

- Centralized P2P network such as Napster
- Decentralized P2P network such as KaZaA
- Structured P2P network such as CAN
- Unstructured P2P network such as Gnutella

Kazaa uses peer-to-peer technology. This means that individual users connect to each other directly, without need for a central point of management. All you need to do is install Kazaa and it will connect you to other Kazaa users. For example Peter downloads Kazaa and installs it onto his computer. Mary also has Kazaa installed on her computer. Peter uses Kazaa to search for a file he is looking for. Kazaa finds the file on Mary's computer. Peter can now download the file directly from Mary.

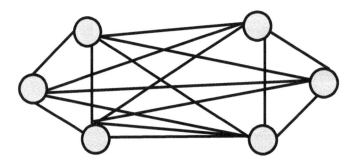

Figure 1.1: Kazaa Networking

The Kazaa software allows you to:

- Search and download content that is shared by premium content providers or by other Kazaa users.
- 'Kreate' your own files and distribute them using Kazaa. Find out more about how to 'Kreate' and Share your own files.

> ➤ The P2P Searches occur through users with fast connections, called Super nodes. Once located, the file is sourced for downloading directly from the user who has it. Find out more about Super nodes.

It is important to ensure that you carefully choose which files you want to share. Don't share files which are personal, such as financial information, or which you do not have the right to distribute.

1.3 PEER-TO-PEER NETWORKING SCENARIOS

Peer-to-peer networking enables or enhances the following scenarios:

> ➤ Real-time communications (RTC)
> ➤ Collaboration
> ➤ Content distribution
> ➤ Distributed processing
> ➤ Improved Internet technologies

1.3.1 Real-Time Communications (RTC)

For RTC, peer-to-peer networking enables server less instant messaging and real-time matchmaking and game play.

> ➤ Server less instant messaging: RTC exists today. Computer users can chat and have voice or video conversations with their peers today. However, many of the existing programs and their communications protocols rely on servers to function. If you are participating in an ad-hoc wireless network or are a part of an isolated network, you are unable to use these RTC facilities. Peer-to-peer technology allows the extension of RTC technologies to these additional networking environments.
> ➤ Real-time matchmaking and game play: Similar to RTC, real-time game play exists today. There are many Web-based game sites that cater to the gaming community via the Internet. They offer the ability to find other gamers with similar interests and play a game together. The problem is that the game sites exist only on the Internet and are geared toward the avid gamer who wants to play against the best gamers in the world. These sites track and provide the statistics to help in the process. However, these sites do not allow a gamer to set up an ad-hoc game among friends in a variety of networking environments. Peer-to-peer networking can provide this capability.

1.3.2 Collaboration

For collaboration, peer-to-peer networking allows the sharing of a workspace, files, and experiences. An example of a collaboration-based Windows Peer-to-Peer Networking application is Windows Meeting Space, which is included in Windows Vista. For more information, see Windows Meeting Space.

> ➤ Project workspaces solving a goal: Shared workspace applications allow for the creation of ad-hoc workgroups and then allow the workgroup owners to populate the shared workspace with the tools and content that will allow the group to solve a problem. This could include message boards, productivity tools, and files.
> ➤ Sharing your files with other people: A subset of project workspace sharing is the ability to share files. Although this ability exists today with the current version of Windows, it can be enhanced through peer-to-peer networking to make file content available in an easy and friendly way. Allowing easy access to the incredible wealth of content at the edge of the Internet or in ad-hoc computing environments increases the value of network computing.

> Sharing your experiences: With wireless connectivity becoming more prevalent, peer-to-peer networking allows you to be online in a group of peers and to be able to share your experiences (such as a sunset, a rock concert, or a vacation cruise) while they are occurring.

1.3.3 Content Distribution

Peer-to-peer networking allows the distribution of text, audio, and video and software product updates.

> Text messages: Peer-to-peer networking can allow for the dissemination of text-based information in the form of files or messages to a large group of users. An example is a news list.
> Audio and video: Peer-to-peer networking can also allow for the dissemination of audio or video information to a large group of users, such as a large concert or company meeting. To distribute the content today, you must configure high-capacity servers to collect and distribute the load to hundreds or thousands of users. With peer-to-peer networking, only a handful of peers would actually get their content from the centralized servers. These peers would flood this information out to a few more people who send it to others, and so on. The load of distributing the content is distributed to the peers in the cloud. A peer that wants to receive the content would find the closest distributing peer and get the content from them.
> Distribution of product updates: Peer-to-peer networking can also provide an efficient mechanism to distribute software such as product updates (security updates and service packs). A peer that has a connection to a software distribution server can obtain the product update and propagate it to the other members of its group.

1.3.4 Distributed Processing

Peer-to-peer networking allows computing tasks to be distributed and processor resources to be aggregated.

> Division and distribution of a task: A large computing task can first be divided into separate smaller computing tasks well suited to the computing resources of a peer. A peer could do the dividing of the large computing task. Then, peer-to-peer networking can distribute the individual tasks to the separate peers in the group. Each peer performs its computing task and reports its result back to a centralized accumulation point.
> Aggregation of computer resources: Another way to utilize peer-to-peer networking for distributed processing is to run programs on each peer that run during idle processor times and are part of a larger computing task that is coordinated by a central server. By aggregating the processors of multiple computers, peer-to-peer networking can turn a group of peer computers into a large parallel processor for large computing tasks.

1.3.5 Improved Internet Technologies

Peer-to-peer networking can also provide an improved utilization of the Internet and support new Internet technologies. Historically, the Internet was designed so that network peers can have end-to-end connectivity. The modern-day Internet, however, more closely resembles a client/server environment where communication in many cases is not end-to-end due to the prevalence of Network Address Translators (NATs).

The user must first download and execute a peer-to-peer networking program. (Gnutellanet is currently one of the most popular of these decentralized P2P programs because it allows users to exchange all types of files.) After launching the program, the user enters the IP address of another computer belonging to the network. (Typically, the Web page where the user got the download will list several IP addresses as places to begin). Once the computer finds another network member on-line, it will connect to that user's connection (who has gotten their IP address from another user's connection and so on).

Users can choose how many member connections to seek at one time and determine which files they wish to share or password protect.

This return to the original purpose of the Internet will enable the creation of a new wave of applications for personal communication and group productivity.

1.4 APPLICATION AREAS

The following are few of the significant applications currently being exercised by incorporating Peer-to-peer networks.

> Bioinformatics: Peer-to-peer networks have also begun to attract attention from scientists in other disciplines, especially those that deal with large datasets such as bioinformatics. P2P networks can be used to run large programs designed to carry out tests to identify drug candidates. The first such program was begun in 2001 the Centre for Computational Drug Discovery at Oxford University in cooperation with the National Foundation for Cancer Research. There are now several similar programs running under the auspices of the United Devices Cancer Research Project. On a smaller scale, a self-administered program for computational biologists to run and compare various bioinformatics software is available from Chinook.

> Education and Academic: Due to the fast distribution and large storage space features, many organizations are trying to apply P2P network for educational and academic purposes. For instance, Pennsylvania State University, MIT and Simon Fraser University are carrying on a project called LionShare designed for facilitating file sharing among educational institutions globally.

> Military: The U.S. Department of Defense has already started research topic on P2P network as part of its modern network war. In May, 2003 Dr. Tether. Director of Defense Advanced Research Project Agency has testified that U.S. Military is using P2P network. Due to security reasons, many files are still kept in confidential.

> Business: P2P network has already been used in business areas, but it is still at the beginning line. Currently, Kato et al's studies indicate over 200 companies with approximately $400 million USD are investing in P2P network. Besides File Sharing, companies are also interested in Distributing Computing, Content Distribution, e-market place, Distributed Search engines, Groupware and Office Automation via P2P network. There are several reasons why companies prefer P2P sometimes such as: Real-time collaboration, a server cannot manage with increasing volume of contents, a process requires strong computing power, a process needs high-speed communications etc. At the same time, P2P is not fully used as it still confronts a lot of security issues.

> TV Telecommunication: Nowadays, people are not just satisfied with "can hear a person from another side of the earth," instead, the demands of clearer voice in real-time are increasing globally. Just like the TV network, there are already cables built. It's not very likely for companies to change all the cables. Many of them turn to use internet, more specifically, P2P network. For instance, Skype, one of the most widely used phone software is using P2P technology. Furthermore, many research organizations are trying to apply P2P network on cellular network.

1.5 DEFINING THE PROBLEM AND THE MOTIVATIONAL FACTORS

This part of the chapter discusses about the problems and the motivational factors that have been identified and in the current study.

➢ Although the problem of data authentication is well digested and practical solutions exist, secure delivery of multimedia streams is challenging due to several reasons. First, the authentication mechanism, which can be computationally expensive, has to keep up with the online nature of streams. Second, multimedia content is often distributed over unreliable channels, where packet losses are not uncommon. The authentication scheme needs to function properly even in presence of these losses. Third, the information added to the streams by the authentication scheme should be minimized in order to avoid increasing the already-high storage and network bandwidth requirements for multimedia content. Finally and most importantly, the authentication scheme must support the flexibility of scalable streams and successfully verify any sub stream extracted from the original stream.

➢ In P2P streaming systems, the upload bandwidths of peers are often far less than their demanded download rates. For example, an average-to-good quality video stream requires about 1–2 Mbps bandwidth, whereas the average upload capacity of home users with DSL and cable connections is often less than a few hundred kbps. To make up for this asymmetry, a number of seed servers need to be deployed in the P2P network in order to deliver high-quality video streams to users. These servers have finite capacity and are often loaded with a volume of requests larger than their serving capacity. Accordingly, arbitrary allocation of these servers for serving peers will result in poor management of resources and inefficient utilization of data, especially when these servers serve scalable video streams

The major problem that the proposed work is concentrated on is malicious payload insertion that is basically a complicated technique of upload a malicious program by various means into the communication channel of multiple P2P clients. The primary goals of malicious payload up loader fall under one of three categories: information dispersion, information harvesting, and information processing. An intruder may not be motivated by these goals and perhaps creates the malicious payload for fun or fame; however, we focus on goals that clearly indicate economic incentive as we believe these goals are the most dangerous. The goal of information dispersion includes sending out spam, creating denial of service attacks, providing false information from illegally controlled sources, etc. The goal of information harvesting includes obtaining identity data, financial data, password data, relationship data (i.e., email addresses of friends), and any other type of data available on the host. The goal of information processing is to process data such as cracking a password stored as a MD5 hash. Such types of malicious payloads will just need basic computing resources to accomplish its goals including CPU cycles, network, memory, and other resources.

1.6 PURPOSE OF THE STUDY

The main purpose of this book chapter is to formulate a robust security technique used in securing multimedia streaming over P2P network considering various threat and attack scenario in order to design a secure and strong networking protocol for protecting the contents in multimedia streaming in maximum attack test bed in P2P networking topology. The secondary aim also includes enhancement of QoS of the multimedia streaming after performing security protocols in proposed model. Following objective were accomplished in the due course of proposed study:

- ➢ To carry out an extensive review of literature for visualizing the prior techniques adopted to mitigate the security loopholes in P2P networks.
- ➢ To introduce a framework for mitigating the request of illegitimate peers in multimedia file sharing in P2P network.
- ➢ Introduced a novel security technique called as Video Streaming Verification Protocol (VSVP) that ensures highly secured transmission of multimedia contents.
- ➢ Considered the potential threat of malicious data insertion that is basically a complicated technique of upload a malicious program by various means into the communication channel of multiple P2P clients.
- ➢ To introduce a framework for secure multimedia transmission in P2P using recurrence relation and evolutionary algorithm.
- ➢ Conducted a performance comparative analysis for the current P2P security developed with previous research models.

1.7 CONCLUSIONS

Although the reminder of this book emphasizes on constructing computational mathematical modelling which is subjected to represent overall framework for efficient and reliable multimedia file transmission in a P2P network, this chapter deals with discussing the preliminary facts which are required to represent conventional security requirements to establish peer-to-peer (P2P) communication for multimedia file-transmission in a client-server model.

REFERENCES

[1]   A.Hamza and A. Kwok, A primer on video streaming over peer-to-peer network's, International Conference on Multimedia and Expo, pp. 1417–1420, 2010

[2]   Almeida, RBD, Vieira, AB, Paula, A & Silva, C 2012, An´alise do Impacto de Ataques de Poluic¸ ˜aoCombinado com Whitewashing emSistemas P2P de Live Streaming

[3]   Amoretti, M 2009 A Survey of Peer-to-Peer Overlay Schemes: Effectiveness, Efficiency and Security, Recent Patents on Computer Science

[4]   An, DS, Ha, B-L &L.Cho, G 2013, A Robust Trust Management Scheme against the Malicious Nodes in Distributed P2P Network, International Journal of Security and Its Applications, vol. 7, no. 3

[5]   Anandaraj, M, Ganeshkumar, P &Vijayakumar, KP 2013, An Efficient QOS Based Multimedia Content Distribution Mechanism in P2P Network, International Journal, vol. 3, no. 5

[6]   Araujo, RD, Ferreira, HNM, Rosa, PF, Gonc, R &Cattelan, A. 2012, A Redundancy Information Protocol for P2P Networks in Ubiquitous Computing Environments: Design and Implementation, International Conference on Networks

CHAPTER 2

OVERVIEW OF CONVENTIONAL SECURITY APPROACHES IN PEER-TO-PEER COMMUNICATION SYSTEM

2.1 OVERVIEW

This part of book has discussed about the different literatures that has been collected in the due course of studies pertaining to mitigation techniques and various standard techniques presented by various researchers in past decade. The content has arranged in the manner of multiple sections and finally, it discusses about the research gap and revealed some important factor to make researcher motivated to evolve with significant solutions to secure and achieve reliable peer to peer network.

2.2 PRIOR TECHNIQUES OF MITIGATION OF ILLEGAL PEER

Nicolas et al. [1] conduct a measurement study of content availability in four of the most popular peer-to-peer file sharing networks, in the absence of poisoning, and then simulate different poisoning strategies on the measured data to evaluate their potential impact.

Ruichuan et al. [2] proposed poisoning-resistant security framework for peer-to-peer content sharing systems which is able to defend against the content poisoning attack effectively and efficiently.

Stephanos [3] has studied current peer-to-peer systems and infrastructure technologies in terms of their distributed object location and routing mechanisms, their approach to content replication, caching and migration, their support for encryption, access control, authentication and identity, anonymity, deniability, accountability and reputation, and their use of resource trading and management schemes.

Dan [4] has proposed a fully functional identity-based encryption scheme (IBE). The scheme has chosen cipher-text security in the random oracle model assuming a variant of the computational Diffie-Hellman problem.

Lei Guo [5] has presented a novel and efficient design of a scalable and reliable media proxy system supported by peer-to-peer networks. This system is called PROP abbreviated from our technical theme of "collaborating and coordinating Proxy and its peer-to-peer clients" with an objective is to address both scalability and reliability issues of streaming media delivery in a cost-effective way.

Ernesto Damiani [6] proposed a self-regulating system where the peer-to-peer network is used to implement a robust reputation mechanism.

Dumitriu [7] considered the file targeted attacks in current use in the Internet, and we introduce a new class of peer-to-peer-network-targeted attacks.

Tom [8] proposed a peer-to-peer protocol that integrates the functions of identification, tracking and sharing of music with those of licensing, monitoring and payment.

Balachander [9] discuss how CDNs are commonly used on the Web and define a methodology to study how well they perform. A performance study was conducted over a period of months on a set of CDN companies employing the techniques of DNS redirection and URL rewriting to balance load among their servers.

Stefan [10] examines content delivery from the point of view of four content delivery systems: HTTP web traffic, the Akamai content delivery network, and Kazaa and Gnutella peer-to-peer file sharing traffic.

Pablo Rodriguez [11] has discussed that although peer-to-peer technology has been widely associated with the distribution of pirated content and has been subject to a barrage of attacks (e.g. DoS, spoofing and content pollution), and there are ways to decrease the risks associated with distributing content using peer-to-peer technology.

Matthew [12] has analyzed the cost of the implementing the redundant task allocation in order to prevent illegal cases over internet. Kevin Walsh [AR] employed a novel voter correlation scheme to weigh the opinions of peers, which gives rise to favorable incentives and system dynamics by presenting simulation results indicating that system is scalable, efficient, and robust.

Runfang Zhou [13] proposes a gossip-based reputation system (GossipTrust) for fast aggregation of global reputation scores which leverages a Bloom filter based scheme for efficient score ranking. GossipTrust does not require any secure hashing or fast lookup mechanism thus is applicable to both unstructured and structured peer-to-peer networks.

Currently, many reputation models have been proposed to address the problem of content poisoning in peer-to-peer content sharing systems. In general, these reputation models can be grouped into three categories: peer-based models, object based models and hybrid models. In peer-based reputation models, e.g., Eigen Trust, Peer Trust and Scrubber, genuine users collectively identify content poisoners by computing a reputation score for each user, and then isolate these poisoners from the system. However, the studies in old research work implied that these peer-based models are insufficient to defend against the poisoning attack.

To address such problems we are going to propose proactive content poisoning system In contrast, our scheme detects unpaid pirates and use discriminatory content poisoning to deter on-line piracy. Legitimate clients can still enjoy the flexibility and convenience provided by open peer-to-peer networks. Our scheme stops pirates from illegal download of copyrighted files, even at the presence of many colluding peers. We developed a reputation-based method to detect peer collusion in piracy process.

2.3 PRIOR TECHNIQUES OF RESISTING PAYLOAD INSERTION

In this section, we present some related work and highlight how our system differs. Several research projects have lead to different systems such as P2VoD [14], GnuStreeam [15], ZigZag [16], Pals [17], Promise [18] but they mainly focus on the overlay level. They present solutions about the way to structure the overlay network: tree or mesh [19] and the way data should be fetched, receiver-driven solution or sender-driven solution.

Some also proposes to take into account the network, via application probes but without relation with network operators. [20], [21] or [22] includes such network-awareness concept as currently under definition in IETF ALTO (Application Level Transport Optimization) group [23] or adaptation but as others, they do not propose watermarking solution to control the contents, neither the system peers concept to monitor the network behavior. There also exist deployed solutions, such as Ray V [24], Peerialism [25], Peering Portal [26] but they do not implement functions for cooperation with network operator, neither watermarking options. Finally, well-known and used solutions [27] [28] such as PPLive, PPStream, TVants for Live content, do not take into consideration the network and do not take care about legality of contents.

Jiehui JU et al. [29] have proposed the multiple attribute decision making problems to evaluate the key technology for peer-to-peer network route security with 2-tuple linguistic information. They extended the TOPSIS model to solve the evaluation problems of key technology for peer-to-peer network route security with 2-tuple linguistic information. According to the traditional ideas of TOPSIS, the optimal alternative(s) is determined by calculating the shortest distance from the 2-tuple linguistic positive ideal solution (TLPIS) and on the other side the farthest distance of the 2-tuple linguistic negative ideal solution (TLNIS)

Rahul J. Vaghela1 et al. [30] have demonstrated that includes the distributed approach defined as Self Certification to Provide the Security in such a Network. In this Paper they have compared these patterns using theoretical analysis and Simulated Network.

Do-sik An et al. [31] have propose a robust trust management scheme to improve reliability and effectiveness of distributed peer-to-peer network by identifying these malicious threats and then limiting the attacker's participation. Especially, their scheme effectively manages for some attacks such as bad mouthing, on-off and sybil. The proposed scheme is expected to effectively protect attacks from malicious peers with improving credibility as well as exactness.

R.Geetha M.E et al. [32] have studied the different streaming services in peer-to-peer environment and also different forwarding mechanisms. They analysed the hybrid-forwarding architecture greatly improves the throughput, and also analysed security issues and trust models.

A. Suganya et al. [33] have presented self-certification, an identity management mechanism, reputation model, and a cryptographic protocol that facilitates generation of global reputation data in a peer-to-peer network, in order to expedite detection of rogues. The self-certification-based identity generation mechanism reduces the threat of liar farms by binding the network identity of a peer to his real-life identity while still providing him anonymity.

R. SuneelManohar et al. [34] have presents an Integrated file Replication and consistency Maintenance mechanism (IRM). Integrated file Replication and consistency Maintenance mechanism integrates the two techniques in a systematic and harmonized manner. The security has become one of the major issues for data communication over worldwide networks. Currently many number of people using the internet. With the lack of security the data may be hacked. So in this they are introducing the routers in between the replica nodes and clients. Which protects sensitive information from unauthorized access? This routers provides security The main objective of the paper is to propose a dynamic routing with security considered using strongest algorithm, such as Blow fish algorithm which is a provide the strong security from the client to the server system.

ZiedTrifa and **Maher Khemakhem** [35] have attempted to provide a taxonomy of structured peer-to-peer overlay networks security attacks. They have specially focused on the way these attacks can arise at each level of the network. Moreover, they observed that most of the existing systems such as Content Addressable Network (CAN), Chord, Pastry, Tapestry, Kademlia, and Viceroy suffer from threats and vulnerability which lead to disrupt and corrupt their functioning. They hope that their survey constitutes a good help for who's working on this area of research.

Stephen S Kirkman et al. [36] have demonstrated a peer-to-peer security should be of interest to anyone who wants to protect their personal information and who actively uses the Internet. Peer-to-peer Security has been a popular research topic for as long as peer-to-peer computing came into existence nearly a decade ago. Peer-to-peer file sharing applications still remain popular and other applications based onpeer-to-peer networks have gained in popularity.

Benjamin Schleinzer et al. [37] have showed how even with limited own resources large amounts of data can be distributed to a wide user base while insuring the integrity of the disseminated data. The data is split into chunks and for each chunk a hash is computed. The initial service provider only communicates the computed hashes and individual chunks are downloaded directly from other peers.

Tien Tuan AnhDinh and Mark Ryan [38] have focus on structured peer-to-peer overlays, in which peers form rigid topologies, i.e. a node only connects to a certain set of neighbours. Examples are Chord, Pastry, etc. It is necessary to update the topology when nodes join or leave the network, which is an expensive operation.

Exact-match searching is done deterministically and is very efficient. In many overlays, it takes O(logN) hops, where N is the number of peers.

Michele Amoretti [39] have designed a categorization for the peer-to-peer overlay schemes and a survey of the most popular ones, comparing each other with respect to effectiveness and security. Most of them have been or are being used in content sharing systems that over the last few years have enjoyed explosive popularity. Others are used in parallel and distributed computing, massively multi-player gaming, Internet streaming, ambient intelligence, etc. Considering such a wide range of applications, they discuss the importance of reputation management in supporting trust management among peer participants.

Markus Fiedler et al. [40] have propose how to parameter and maintain a reputation system that, based on the current network conditions, supports the selection of the optimal communication end-to-end path for VoIP communication in peer-to-peer network. Each node's reputation is formed based on three factors: (1) performance reputation (own experience from passive measures of the network conditions); (2) security reputation; and (3) information reputation consisting of recommendations from other nodes. Reputation data is periodically updated from continuous lightweight monitoring of path quality and security and also from information exchange between the nodes.

Miguel Castro et al. [41] have studied attacks aimed at preventing correct message delivery in structured peer-to-peer overlays and presents defences to these attacks. They describe and evaluate techniques that allow nodes to join the overlay, to maintain routing state, and to forward messages securely in the presence of malicious nodes.

Nithya et.al [42] has studied study the different streaming services in peer-to-peer environment and also different forwarding mechanisms.

Mokhtarian et.al [43] has studied the problem of managing the seed server capacity in peer-to-peer streaming systems with scalable videos. Using their allocation algorithm, they developed an analytical model to analyze the performance of peer-to-peer streaming systems with scalable videos.

Singh et.al [44] has described the login screen is successfully made.

SakthiSudhan et.al [45] has investigated application layered protocols to the quality of metric values of H.323 protocol video streaming transmission over peer to peer link in wireless scenario.

Filipe et.al [46] have described the peer-to-peer applications became very popular, not only for content sharing and distribution but also for media streaming.

Dittrichet.al [47] analyzed the incentive mechanisms of e-Mule and Bit-Torrent by introducing an abstract classification of incentive mechanisms.

Araujo at.al [48] has presented CAL, a peer-to-peer-based protocol designed to transfer multimedia information captured by different types of devices installed in instrumented environments.

Kumar et.al [49] have illustrated about the peer-to-peer (PEER-TO-PEER) networks continue to be popular means of trading content.

Liu et.al [50] have proposed and experimentally demonstrated a novel peer-to-peer interconnection architecture in a 60-GHz mm-wave RoF access network for the first time. Based on previously developed work, they expose the cause, of peer-to-peer's lack of success in the commercial sector, as techno-economical, rather than just technical, as it is intimately connected to the enforced business models. Hence, it can be seen although couple of researches has been conducted on the same area, but still optimal result is yet to come.

2.4 EXISTING SECURITY TECHNIQUES

In this section we offer an in-depth on the prevailing security solutions in peer-to-peer streaming. We tend to expose and discuss the vulnerabilities of every approach and then derive many patterns and conclusions that may facilitate in protecting against attacks in peer-to-peer streaming systems.

Figure 2.1: Important structural aspects in securing peer-to-peer streaming

As shown in Fig. 2.1, there are 2 building blocks of peer-to-peer systems to be considered: overlay topology and information dissemination mechanisms. The topology of the overlay defines the way to connect every node within the network with the proper neighbours; in different words, in an exceedingly scenario during which nodes are constantly joining and leaving the system, to search out an answer during which every node sees as its neighbours solely the nodes it's most interested (and is fair) to speak with. The factors to settle on neighbour vary from locality to sure QoS values. The topology of the overlay is in tight reference to the applying: the application domain determines the topology of the network, whereas in its flip the overlay topology influences runtime application aspects which will be either useful or non-functional: looking out, routing, performance, efficiency, robustness, [51], [52]. In complicated applications, where the topology changes dynamically, the mechanisms concerned within the construction of the overlay have increased importance as a result of their invoked continuously; consequently, keeping these mechanisms protected against attacks becomes essential so as to keep up their compliance with the protocol schemes. According to several classification studies [53, 54, 55, 56] that there are two typical overlay topologies in peer-to-peer streaming applications:

1. **Tree-overlays**: in which the overlay is typically inbuilt the form of a tree. This implies that the approach during which overlay nodes send and receives messages is structured and embedded within the overlay topology: The supply is that the root of the tree and leaf nodes receive however not redistribute the info. alternative structured topologies, like multi-trees and hypercube exist;

2. **Mesh-overlays**: where the overlay doesn't have a particular structure however it's a generic mesh. That is, each peer has many neighbours, however while not a transparent parent-child relationship or any predefined topology. The media is distributed among totally different peers and then every of them transmits the media any.

Apart from the overlay construction, the opposite defining facet of peer-to-peer systems is that the knowledge dissemination mechanism among peers. That is, whereas the overlay deals with connecting a node with the correct neighbours, the info dissemination algorithm thinks about with the way to choose neighbours to really exchange information with. There are 2 basic ways that of disseminating knowledge in peer-to-peer streaming systems [57]:

1. The push, or source-driven approach means a peer transmits a bit to its neighbours, assuming they are doing not have it yet; the directions during which the info is shipped are determined by the parent-child relationship among nodes, be it a tree or mesh overlays. it's simple to ascertain this manner of performing knowledge dissemination is liable to redundant pushes and therefore to DoS attacks (e.g., flooding neighbours with knowledge they already have), to neighbours choice and omission attacks (bias in where to push data);

2. The pull, or receiver-driven approach is another to the previous theme, by that a peer uses buffer maps to make pull schedule with the peers it decides to speak with. A peer requests the knowledge it's missing. This approach is a lot of strong than the previous, however liable to collusion: peers that have already got knowledge might not advertise it to others.

The data-driven approach is in practice a pull mechanism.

Epidemic algorithms (and gossiping ones in particular) are samples of this approach. Gossip in peer-to-peer could be an information dissemination mechanism that doesn't accept the overlay structure however, autonomously manages its own distribution patterns. It's conjointly helpful in information aggregation and resource allocation [65]. The explanation for its popularity is that gossiping mechanisms are straightforward and additional strong than others. Security-wise, we have a tendency to believe they're attention-grabbing to check as a result of their additional general than the push and pull mechanisms.

The biasing vulnerabilities suffered by the opposite approaches are simply solved with gossip, since it's not simply predictable during which manner information flows. Additionally, as previously noted [64], gossip-based mechanisms are less sensitive to see dynamics, so to churn. For the explanations on top of, in what follows we are going to analyse the 2 overlay approaches in conjunction with gossiping protocols from a security standpoint. We are going to bring into lightweight what are the vulnerabilities and strengths induced to the systems that adopt these approaches.

2.5 TREE-BASED APPROACHES

Generally, streaming in tree-based overlays imposes that the supply of the media is that the root of the tree, which the remainder of the peers are source of the supply and children/parents among themselves. The trail that the information should follow during this case is fixed: initial from the supply to the first-order oldsters, then from those to their kids, and so on. A clear useful drawback that happens with this sort of overlay structure is simple: the potency of the hierarchy is overcome by the massive imbalance between parent nodes and leaf nodes (parents forward information whereas leaves don't, thus everyone needs to be a leaf).

Traditionally, the answer to the current issue took the shape of multi-tree overlays, as [63] notice, in different words: a lot of trees, a lot of leaves. This approach results in distributing the information in multiple distinct trees.

There are different issues associated with the topology of this overlay [62], and that they are summarized in Table 2.1. Since in tree overlays every node receives information from only 1 supply node, bandwidth fluctuations is highly damaging, and methods that are nearer to the basis are a lot of seemingly to show into bottlenecks. Security wise, minor protocol deviations of single nodes will have an effect on simply entire sub trees. Additionally, when nodes nearer to the basis leave the system (e.g., they crash or are attacked), they leave un-serviced an oversized proportion of the nodes.

Generally, streaming in tree-based overlays imposes that the source of the media is the root of the tree, and that the rest of the peers are children of the source and children/parents among themselves. The path that the data must follow in this case is fixed: first from the source to the first-order parents, then from those to their children, and so on. A visible functional problem that occurs with this kind of overlay structure is simple: the efficiency of the hierarchy is overcome by the large imbalance between parent nodes and leaf nodes (parent's forward data while leaves do not, so everybody wants to be a leaf). Historically, the solution to this issue took the form of multi-tree overlays, as [63] notice, in other words: more trees, more leaves. This approach leads to distributing the data in multiple distinct trees. There are other problems related to the topology of this overlay [63], and they are summarized in Table 2.1. Since in tree overlays each node receives data from only one source node, bandwidth fluctuations can be highly damaging, and paths that are closer to the root are more likely to turn into bottlenecks. Security wise, minor protocol deviations of single nodes can affect easily entire sub trees. Additionally, when nodes closer to the root leave the system (e.g., they crash or are attacked), they leave subserviced a large percentage of the nodes.

Table 2.1: Common fairness and security issues in tree-based peer-to-peer streaming systems

Problem/attacks	Envisaged solutions
- Imbalance root vs. leafs - Bandwidth fluctuation, bottleneck, - Protocol deviation on parent node	Using multi-trees, gossip
- Identifying malicious nodes, DoS, - omission, membership attacks	Monitor, acknowledgement
Forgery, repudiation	Signatures
Sybil attacks	Not yet solved.

Attempting to unravel the higher than issues, Zhou and Liu have combined the tree overlay with gossip knowledge dissemination so the 2 approaches would compensate every other's faults [63]. As a result of the tree model is brittle however nonetheless time-efficient, it is used as a second option: by default all knowledge is transmitted by gossiping, and if a node doesn't receive something for a particular amount of your time, the tree overlay are going to be used to get the info from its parent. Security-wise, as a result of the protection level for a composite system is that the protection level of its weakest link, this resolution is liable to all vulnerabilities of the tree overlay. Another resolution adopted in tree-based overlays is presented by Shetty et al. in [65]. In tree-shaped overlays, the streaming quality depends on the cooperation of the non-leaf nodes (namely the nodes within the overlay tree that are neither leaves nor the source). The potential attacks that are thought of are therefore DoS, omission, forgery and repudiation attacks. Shetty et al. establish that one in all the issues with this security solution in peer-to-peer streaming is that they can't establish the malicious nodes themselves, simply the very fact that there are malicious nodes. this can be as a result of in overlay multicast streaming, if a good peer receives tampered knowledge, it cannot confirm if its parent is malicious (since its parent may need taken that knowledge from another peer).

Signed acknowledgments beside a random monitoring theme were shown to be an answer to detect the precise attacker peers. The previous mechanism is employed by peers to prove their fairness, whereas the latter helps trusted peers to watch during a random fashion a number of their peers suspected to malfunction. The matter with this answer style is that it depends on one single session trust manager that imposes a scalability issue and one purpose of failure. The trust manager decides whether or not a peer is malicious or not, by receiving 'complaints' from peers and using a localization theme. If it cannot detect the precise location of the omission or forgery attack, the trust manager can decrease the trust worth of each peer (the reporter and therefore the reported). Otherwise, the child node and therefore the tree that inherit from the reported node are moved to a different peer-tree.

2.6 MESH-BASED APPROACHES

Mesh-shaped overlays are less structured as compared to the tree solutions. A membership server could keep track of the prevailing nodes within the system if needed, and there's no fastened flow that knowledge should follow. Recent works see these meshes as unidirectional, within the sense that nodes have separated inbound and outbound links. The quantity of neighbors that a node will settle for is proscribed by resources or by the protocol. Empirically, a comparison between multi-tree and mesh-based overlays in streaming eventualities is given in [62, 63] and also the conclusion is that mesh approaches are additional strong. The study shows that overlays that are mesh-shaped bear higher performance when the scale of the network is massive, the streaming rates are high, and also the nodes have high bandwidth and low round-trip times. On the drawback, they'll introduce an oversized range of duplicate packets within the network. Multi-trees, as compared, are additional time-efficient in heterogeneous networks; however on massive scales they perform worse than meshes. Some problems with the mesh-based overlay are shown in Table 2.2.

Two classical examples in mesh-based overlay solutions are prime [66] and Cool Streaming [67]. In Cool Streaming, the approach is data-driven: the info availability drives additional propagation; gossip communication is employed to disseminate network membership and content availability. Building on Cool Streaming, that doesn't type a typical mesh however many trees onto an initial mesh, Prime is traditionally one amongst the primary mesh streaming systems. In Prime, content delivery (or swarming) has 2 phases: push reporting is finished by oldsters (announcing availability of knowledge) and pull-reporting by youngsters (retrieving data using some packet scheduling algorithm). For advertising the new content dedicated links are in place (diffusion connections) over diffusion trees.

Table 2.2: Common security issues in mesh-based peer-to-peer streaming systems, and possible solutions

Problem	Envisaged Solutions
Identifying malicious nodes Flooding, omission attacks, Membership Attacks	Monitor and audit schemes
Collusion attacks, data diffusion issues, acknowledgment / Repudiation problems	Not yet solved

From a security purpose of read, neither Prime nor Cool Streaming defend themselves from effects of many sorts of attacks. As an example, Prime assumes that peers are all honest and connect in a very random fashion with each other, which the mesh fashioned by peers is directed. Since there's no mechanism to examine whether or not rather than randomness, some nodes will connect solely to sure different nodes on purpose, therefore coalitions (and additionally network partitioning) will type. Aside from the easy collusion attack, the integrity of the diffusion connections isn't enforced. There's no mechanism in place to create positive that one node declares its content availability to all or any or none or a fraction of its neighbours; there's no guarantee that the bandwidth, outgoing and ingoing degree of every node are used properly. Even additional importantly, there's the problem of acknowledgement and repudiation: there's no guarantee that peers eventually receive streamed knowledge.

2.7 MISCELLENOUS TECHNIQUES

Muller et al. [68] have presented experiments with efficient Content Based Image Retrieval in a peer-to-peer environment, thus a peer-to-peer-CBIR system. Although according to the work, peer data summaries can be used within the retrieval process for increasing efficiency, but security aspects are ignored.

Jung and Cho [69] have proposed a watermarking platform for protecting unauthorized content distribution in peer-to-peer networks. The proposed platform dynamically generates 2D barcode watermark according to consumer's data and inserts the watermark into downloaded audio source in wavelet domain. However, the proposed watermarking platform is not able to prohibit illegal usage of digital audio content.

Chu et al. [70] have investigated the requirements for multimedia content sharing among peer-to-peer networks and proposed a novel business models along with Digital Rights Management (DRM) solutions. The aim of this DRM research is to set new business models for content owners to benefit from the massive power of content distribution of peer-to-peer networks with least intrusion and interference to end consumer's privacy and anonymity.

Kumar and Sivaprakasam [71] have proposed a new encryption mechanism is included in which a message is transformed into a binary image which cannot be identified as a cipher text or stegno object. The approach is very much better for transmitting a confidential data from client to server. However, peer-to-peer network reliability is not ensured as the experiments were performed on adhoc network.

Mathieu et al. [72] have proposed a peer-to-peer system that ensures the security of contents, by controlling that only authorized contents are exchanged between peers and by being able to identify the people that redistribute illegal contents if it happens. This is mostly addressed by the use of watermarking functions in the video contents processing and by the deployment of specific peers that can monitor and detect misbehavior of the peers.

Meddour et al. [73] have performed a study where the authors have investigated various available techniques that uses the potential features of peer-to-peer techniques for enhancing the existing multimedia streaming protocols. The author specified that current open issues in multimedia peer-to-peer streaming are a) appropriate video coding scheme, b) managing peer dynamicity, c) peer heterogeneity, d) efficient overlay network construction, e) selection of the best peers, f) monitoring of network conditions, and g) incentives for participating peers.

Berson [74] has discussed the security aspects of Skype. Tang et al. [75] have proposed their work on real-time peer-to-peer application for live multimedia streaming termed as Grid Media that was used for broadcasting real-time events over the internet.

Hughes and Walkerdine [75] have discussed their work on distributed multimedia encoding techniques as a tool to exploit the extra-computational resources of standing computing devices using peer-to-peer network.

Reforgiato et al. [76] have presented their work that uses multiple point for broadcasting their multimedia contents over heterogeneous content distribution peer-to-peer networking system. The authors have used MPEG-4 encoder without any losses at the base layer stream.

Hagemeister [77] has described the framework for a distributed censorship-resistant policy drafting system. By relying on a DTN as well as a peer-to-peer network, the system can work even without internet access.

We have attempted to explore some prior work done towards securing image or video contents over peer-to-peer network and examined some attacks and issues with peer-to-peer networks. In the multimedia content distribution scenario, this server is usually hosted and maintained by the content providers. This results in peer user's anonymity interference and content provider's efforts in server maintenance. It was found that majority of the work done past is either on cryptography or using DRM or watermarking, where the prime concern is the privacy and anonymity issues of content consumers. Since DRM systems track user transactions, purchases, and access history, end consumers' detail activities are recorded at content retailer's database and thus raise divergences regarding multimedia content protection versus privacy protection. Due to the inherent characteristics of decentralization, peer-to-peer network suffers from security loopholes as there is no central monitoring or control system to mitigate the online threats or attacks. No much work towards securing image or video content while transmission is explored very recently or even in past.

2.8 EXPLICIT TECHNQIUES TO SECURE PEER-TO-PEER NETWORK

This section discusses about the most prominent literatures that has been critically reviewed for the purpose of carrying out the proposed investigation in security system of multimedia content over vulnerable peer-to-peer network.

Ha et al. [73] developed simple mathematical representations of the cost characteristics of two internet video distribution systems: Content Delivery Networks (CDNs) and peer-to-peer networks and identify conditions under which each or a blend of the two proves most cost-effective. Their analysis shows that in many cases a hybrid system is likely to have lower costs than either a pure CDN or a pure peer-to-peer network.

Kalaivani and **Saisaranya** [74] investigate the unique properties of forums based on the data collected from the Disney discussion boards. According to these properties, to design a scheme to support peer-to-peer-based multimedia sharing in forums called Multimedia Board (MBoard). MBoard can significantly reduce the load on the server while maintaining a high quality of service for the users and also this MBoard system toward the application of peer-to-peer-based multimedia sharing in forums or other mediums used to deliver user generated multimedia content.

Mottalib et al. [75] performed a comparative study among three pollution defense mechanisms in peer-to-peer live streaming systems. The paper also proposes a combined mechanism which is showing a better result to restrict the pollution.

Ozturk and **Clincy** [76] proposed the basis for a study in quantitatively understanding the effect in deploying various combinations of video encoding and network coding approaches on peer-to-peer streaming systems in a wireless environment. A simulation model will be implemented and used for analyzing the video traffic and its flow through the network.

Almeida et al. [77] address attacks in a peer-to-peer system. More precisely, they analyze a reputation system in a mesh based peer-to-peer system under a pollution attack. During the attack, malicious users collude and also change their identities (whitewashing) often trying to cheat the reputation system. They have tested the reputation system on Planet Lab, which confirms it efficiency during an attack without whitewashing.

Anandaraj et al. [78] focused on constructing and maintaining an efficient multiple overlay multicast tree structure in the peer-to-peer network. The tree maintenance process is governed by two mechanisms called as dynamic reconfiguration driven by peer and less frequent tree maintenance by network status change observation. In this paper new scalable architecture is constructed and analyzed based on the above strategies.

Chu et al. [79] presented, the requirements for multimedia content sharing among peer-to-peer (PEER-TO-PEER) networks are investigated and novel business models along with Digital Rights Management (DRM) solutions are proposed. In the current approach, to provide least intrusion and interference for end content consumers, content providers are not involved in the communications or peer transactions of peer-to-peer networks after the multimedia content are sold to the peer users.

Pakstas et al. [80] proposed an optimized design of a peer-to-peer-based VoD system, VoDP Stream, resorting to peer-to-peer computing for its remarkable performance in data distribution and Gossip Protocol which helps to construct a dynamic network overlay. A modified algorithm has been worked out to realize fine performance and promoted efficiency in information management, buffer management and node operation.

Mathieu et al. [81] presented a solution for mitigating illegal contents, distributed in a video streaming peer-to-peer network. The main goal of this study was to convince content providers that a solution to protect them against illegal distribution exists. Indeed, while DRM protections are often seen as a major drawback of legal distribution platforms (because the technologies are not compatible with each other, or with some devices, or players and sometimes prohibit legitimate uses of content), the watermarking technology they use is a transparent form of protection for video.

Lin et al. [82] focused on providing incentives for user cooperation. They propose a game-theoretic framework to model user behavior and to analyze the optimal strategies for user cooperation simulation in wireless video streaming. They first analyze the Pareto optimality and the time-sensitive bargaining equilibrium of the two-person game. They then extend the solution to the multiuser scenario.

Neysiani et al. [83] proposed, the efficiency of the pull based exchange method in mesh-based peer-to-peer live video streaming is analyzed and examined for different peer churning rates, network sizes, initial buffer times, BMS (Buffer Map Status) exchange interval times and heterogeneous bandwidth. Moreover, a trade-off between the BMS message interval time and the network overhead in pull-based method is evaluated in order to clearly show why most of the previous studies used one second BMS interval time.

Aguirre et al. [84] propose an original method to geoposition an audio/video stream with multiple emitters that are at the same time receivers of the mixed signal. The achieved method is suitable for those comes where a list of positions within a designated area is encoded with a degree of precision adjusted to the visualization capabilities; and is also easily extensible to support new requirements.

Favalli et al. [85] proposed a content delivery system for real-time streaming services based on a peer-to-peer approach that exploits multicast overlay organization of the peers to address the challenges due to bandwidth heterogeneity. To improve reliability and flexibility, video is coded using a scalable multiple description approach that allows delivery of sub-streams over multiple trees and allows rate adaptation along the trees as the available bandwidth changes.

Trifa and **Khemakhem** [86] attempted to provide taxonomy of structured peer-to-peer overlay networks security attacks. They have specially focused on the way these attacks can arise at each level of the network. Moreover, they observed that most of the existing systems such as Content Addressable Network (CAN), Chord, Pastry, Tapestry, Kademlia, and Viceroy suffer from threats and vulnerability which lead to disrupt and corrupt their functioning.

Some of the recent survey of the existing research work based on streaming issues in peer-to-peer network is shown in Table 2.3.

Table 2.3: Survey on Recent Researches on Security on peer-to-peer streaming

Author	Problem	Approach used
William et.al [87] 2006	- Selfishness - Denial-of-service attacks	- Oversight framework
Ratan and Darshan [88] 2006	- Free rider's Attack - Whitewasher's Attack - Malicious payload insertion attacks	- Lightweight integrity
Maya and Robbert [89] 2007	- DoS - Forgery, membership, omission attacks	- Live-streaming malicious behavior
William and Klara [90] 2007	- Subset of trusted peers (called kantoku nodes), throttle attackers	- Selfish nodes and malicious nodes
Xiaoyun Liu et.al [91] 2007	- Data - Encryption and authentication schemes,	- Digital Rights Management (DRM)
Hao Yin et.al [92]	- Security, scalability, heterogeneity, and - Certain QoS	- Trust Stream, a novel, secure and scalable media streaming - CDN and peer-to-peer network
W. Sabrina [93]	- Nash equilibrium - Pareto optimality - Selfish users - Attacking behavior	- Game-theoretic framework - User behavior - Designs incentive-based strategies
Jan Seedorf [94]	- Secure routing, prevention of unsolicited communication, emergency calls, - Distributed user authentication, and privacy considerations.	- Highly distributed and lacking centralized, trusted entities for bootstrapping security mechanisms,
Bertrand et.al [95]	- Legal contents - Overload network	- Video watermarking
Mikko and Janne [96]	- Bandwidth fluctuation - Terminal capabilities	- SVC transmission

Author	Problem	Approach used
Ahmed and Adrian [97]	- Prevent possible attacks from malicious users - Simple attacks (Ripple-Stream) - Aggregate attacks (Kantoku framework)	- Tree and mesh-based systems
Istemi et.al [98]	- Denying video requests by peers and assure that each participant peer	- Multi-objective optimization approach and corresponding for- mutations for the optimal operation of the system.
Hareesh and Manjaiah [99] 2011	- Media streaming, - Live and Video on demand systems	- Dynamic movie replication - replacement, and scheduling
Tsao-Ta Wei et.al [100]	- Scalability, privacy	- SIPTVMON, SIP signaling and AES encryption

Research on security for peer-to-peer streaming started to flourish, but no comprehensive security analysis over the current peer-to-peer solutions has yet been attempted. There are no best practices in system design, no (widely) accepted attack models [101], no measurement-based studies on security threats to peer-to-peer neither streaming, nor even general surveys investigating specific security aspects for these systems.

Compared with the widely used file-sharing networks, peer-to-peer streaming networks are more vulnerable to various attacks for the following reasons. 1) Streaming, especially video streaming, usually requires high bandwidth. A certain amount of data loss could make the whole stream useless. 2) Streaming applications require their data to be delivered in a timely fashion. Data with a missed deadline are useless. 3) A streaming network usually consists of a limited number (sometimes only one) of data sources. The failure of the data source could bring down the whole streaming system. Currently we are not aware of any systematic study on large scale attacks and defenses specifically targeting peer-to-peer streaming networks

2.9 RESEARCH GAP

After reviewing the literatures that discusses about different mitigation techniques against security loopholes for transmitting multimedia contents in peer-to-peer network, following research gap has been extracted.

➢ Majority of the significant literatures e.g. [73][84][75] discusses the usage of content delivery network along with peer-to-peer network. The studies has discusses some of the effective mathematical modeling to put forward a cost effective security solution. But a closer look in such studies will find the lack of inclusion of authentication protocols to be incorporated over the multimedia files to render safety while in transmission cycle. Although effective against DoS attack, but majority of the studies are found to have fluctuated security outcomes. Hence less focus is laid on the illegitimate peer request.

➢ Cryptography has played a significant role in majority of the studies e.g. [91][92][100] etc, however, very few studies has been witness to optimize the encryption technique considering the lethal attacks in peer-to-peer network.

➢ Efficient parameters e.g. packet delivery ratio, number of unauthorized peer request, bandwidth consumption, inter-packet delay were deemed low significance while evaluation of security protocols.

2.10 OVERVIEW OF SECURITY ISSUES IN PEER-TO-PEER NETWORK

Finding real-world examples of security attacks to peer-to-peer streaming systems is (unfortunately?) not easy, because these systems are young and most of all because the organizations managing them are not so keen in releasing information about attacks to their systems. In the following we sketch two examples based on real life events that are clearly related to peer-to-peer streaming and help us introduce the reason why we consider important addressing security issues in peer-to-peer streaming systems and do it before large scale attacks make the headlines of non-technical literature.

2.10.1 Example 1: The Reason for Polluting

Albeit rarely admitted or clearly proved, it is commonly accepted that in file-sharing applications content pollution, i.e., intentionally change parts of the file to make it useless or of bad quality, is a day-by-day routine. In [102] and [103] it is practically given for granted that a peer-to-peer streaming system can undergo pollution attacks. It is often reported that pollution attacks in file sharing are due to the fact that the system is devoted to illegally exchanging copyrighted material, and it is the copyright owner who pollutes the system as a last means to defend its rights when any legal action failed. If this were the situation, then one may think that in a system distributing legal content like standard public TV there is no reason to consider pollution. This position is however rather naïve. Making some specific content unavailable can be a goal for many actors. For instance changing the advertisements on very popular events can lead to very remunerative commercial frauds. On a larger scale, selectively changing (or simply removing) parts of some content may lead to public opinion manipulation that, if done by a government or similar body can be called censorship, but if done by private (criminal) organizations raises even more frightening scenarios.

2.10.2 Example 2: Skype Outage

In recent years, the problem of facilitating signaling in VoIP (Voice over IP) networks through a peer-to-peer network has been subject of intense activity in both research [104] and standardization [105]. While clearly the problem domain is different from video streaming, they share similar security concerns, among which time-sensitiveness is the most important. One of the main attacks that can be played against peer-to-peer VoIP systems is denial of service against the availability of the signaling system: the attacker may try to block the ability for a caller to identify the current location for the designated caller. Furthermore, given that the caller expects to retrieve this information in reasonable time in order to start the call, it may be sufficient for the attacker to severely delay the transmission to the location of the called.

To achieve this goal, one of the easiest forms of attack is to try to perturb the routing substrate of the peer-to-peer system, normally based on distributed hash tables like Chord [106] and Pastry [107]. Possible attacks in these cases include Eclipse, Sybil and neighbor selection attacks. An example of the kind of problems that users can expect from VoIP systems, which can be mirrored in the video streaming domain, is exemplified by the Skype two-day outage which occurred on August 2007 [108].

While Skype has denied that this specific event has been caused by malicious activity, blaming instead the "Microsoft Patch Tuesday" (with a large number of machines rebooting at the same time). This is an example of what could happen when nodes in a peer-to-peer streaming service (voice is being streamed here) loose autonomy. The loss of autonomy, which leads to a dependability problem in this case, is due to the dominance of an operating system in correlating nodes. In general, nevertheless, the same problem can be due to any other reason.

2.11 SECURITY CONSIDERATIONS FOR PEER-TO-PEER STREAMING

In any security analysis, it is important to consider all possible generators of attacks (active elements) against possible targets of attacks (passive). In the first category we find peer-to-peer nodes, super nodes and application code, while in the second we include the protocol, the overlay, and the data being transferred. Although the streaming source can also be a possible target, the usual assumption is that the source is trusted, since we have not found any studies on source-level attacks. The application code can be seen as both active (when causes data leakages, or jeopardize data privacy) element, and passive element of attack (when can be directly manipulated for protocol subversion).

An overview of the threat sources and targets in peer-to-peer streaming applications is given in Tables 2.4 and 2.5 and is detailed hereafter. There are three major elements likely to turn into sources of attacks inpeer-to-peer streaming: Peer nodes Malicious or malfunctioning nodes can always alter the protocol behavior. For instance, they may not reply to requests, or may reply generating wrong messages. This can result into biasing the neighbor selection process of another node, thus into network partitioning or even censorship. Censorship has deep consequences: besides the standard legal aspects, a smaller number of users in the overlay implies a poorer quality of the diffusion [109]. From the point of view of QoS, peers can also do delayed forwarding and hence jeopardize once more live streaming and TV systems.

Table 2.4: Common sources of vulnerabilities in peer-to-peer streaming

Active aspect	Influences what	Results into
Peer nodes	PEER-TO-PEER protocol, QoS	partitioning, censorship, delays, isolation
Supernodes	PEER-TO-PEER protocol, QoS	partitioning, censorship, delays, isolationce
Application code	PEER-TO-PEER protocol, data privacy	Censorship, data leaks

Super nodes: Super nodes do not always exist in peer-to-peer applications, but it is envisioned that they can greatly benefit applications requiring large bandwidth and low, constant delays. Super nodes bring similar vulnerabilities to streaming systems as common peer nodes; however, the emphasis is on their higher responsibility in data diffusion: e.g., if super peers do not behave fairly and honestly with all peers, they can bias the service toward preferred users. As a consequence, partitioning and censorship are more stringent at the super node level. Super nodes become even more critical as some projects explore the possibility that they are controlled by ISPs in an effort to make peer-to-peer overlays and IP networks cooperate [110].

Table 2.5: Common attack targets in peer-to-peer streaming

Passive aspect	Influenced by	Results into
Application code	Code provider	Censorship, data leaks
PEER-TO-PEER protocol	Peers, super peers, application code	censor, partition, pollution, partitition, DoS, data leaks
Overlay routing	data privacy, QoS, overlay routing	data leaks, delays, DoS, partitioning, censorship
Distributed data	data integrity	partitioning

Application code Wallach [111] notices that the peer-to-peer code runs with numerous privileges on peer machines: it normally uses the network connection and the local hard drive. When unrestricted, local access and external communication may lead to information leaks or malicious code installed on the local machine that could alter the overall peer-to-peer protocol. The remedy is twofold:

Sand boxing the peer-to-peer application to use just an isolated location on the local drive, and denying operations that are not coherent with the purposes of the peer-to-peer application. The application code poses a particular threat to users' *privacy*, because embedded malware could leak sensitive information to non-authorized recipients. The passive sources of vulnerability that are usually targets of attacks are:

Overlay routing and maintenance Overlay management messages among peers aims at reliability and quality. Secure routing deals with both maintaining secure routing tables, and securely transmitting messages [117]. The data in transit can be sniffed and if the channel is not secure, it can even be leaked or modified. The dispatching of tampered data to fair peers depends on the security of the overlay and neighborhood tables; not only routing can undergo malicious delaying, but also partitioning (sending tainted data to the same peers) and/or censorship (not sending anything to a group of peers).

The peer-to-peer protocol One way or another, the attackers in a peer-to-peer scenario always try to manipulate the protocol to their own advantage, or to the disadvantage of other peers. The peer-to-peer application protocol is at a higher level than the overlay routing mechanism, and manipulates streamed data by correlating a number of aspects: membership mechanism, data scheduling and transmission, identity management, overlay mechanisms, reputation, etc.

Distributed data: Data integrity is essential in streaming and TV systems, because the purpose of the application is liveness. If a TV-channel is re-distributed on the peer-to-peer system but part of the news/programs are altered with some users treated differently from others, this can lead to partitioning, loss of users, and censorship.

2.12 SYSTEM-LEVEL SECURITY GOALS IN PEER-TO-PEER STREAMING

If the threat model identifies the sources of potential jeopardy to the system, the security model and goals identify the aspects of the system that are jeopardized by the threat. In Table 2.6, we split these aspects into system operation, introduced here, and content management, discussed in Section 2.6.

Table 2.6: Desirable security and privacy features for peer-to-peer streaming Systems

Category	System feature
System operation	Reliability, Availability, Dependability, Node Autonomy, Access Control
Content management	Authenticity, Integrity, Non-repudiation, Confidentiality, Anonymity

For what system operation is concerned, we identify the properties listed in the first row of Table 2.6 and discussed in the sequel as those to be granted to streaming systems in the face of threats and attacks. The system security, in the context of streaming system operation, can be identified with the capability of the system not to *fail*. We note that the term *fail* assumes a different flavor in streaming systems, specially for live events, than in other traditional peer-to-peer systems. Indeed, considering a file-sharing application, failure can be identified with the inability to download a file, or at most with the inability to do that in a given time: it does not matter whether the system operates continuously or in bursts, or if the file is downloaded at a regular pace or all of a sudden right before the deadline. To make another example, in telephony applications it is not a security

requirement that all users can talk at the same time (the probability of such an event is considered negligible). In a streaming system, instead, the inability to connect to a stream by *any* user is a failure, even more so if this happens for a very popular and hence important stream, which might lead to user's discrimination.

> *Reliability*: The up-time of the system in steady state is the reliability of the system, and as such it is normally modeled by the mean time between failures (MTBF). Reliability can be a property of a single device or subsystem, a global property of the entire system or, as more suitable for our purposes, it can refer to the vision of the system conditioned to one specific peer or a subset of peers. A single failure, even if recovered, implies loss of reliability. Let us characterize reliability as

$$p = 1 - \frac{1}{MTBF} \tag{2.1}$$

Where MTBF is the number of consecutive requests from a peer before one fails (hence mtbf ≥ 1). Reliability is a desirable feature for security, but asking high reliability to a highly volatile system, like a peer-to-peer overlay, which is designed for resilience rather than resistance is not appropriate, thus the main goal of reaching a certain level ρ' of reliability is ensuring the system high Availability.

> *Availability*: It is the ability of the system to be up and running. A system can be unreliable, yet highly available, simply because recovery from failures is faster than the user/application of the system can detect. In peer-to-peer streaming, for instance, churn can be a source of unreliability, since peers leaving implies that from the point of view of some other peers, a portion of the system (or a given request) has failed. However, topology reconfiguration can be fast enough to avoid the loss of any information at the application, so that the system remains available even from the perspective of peers that are affected by churn. In general terms, we can say that a secure peer-to-peer streaming system must be available with high probability at any time, contrary to other (not all)peer-to-peer applications, most notably file sharing, where the system can be unavailable for relatively long periods, but still operate securely in that it yields its services.

> *Dependability*: Even if highly available, a system may still suffer from correlated failures that make it non-dependable. Dependability is a subtler property of the system: it reflects the ability of a system to work and provide services in critical moments. An example will clarify the point. Cellular telephone systems are in general reliable and available, however they are not dependable with respect to emergencies and civil protection: during accidents the cells covering the area of the accident become congested because people call with higher rate than normal and resources are locally insufficient; during natural disasters, besides the above phenomenon, normally the electricity fails, and the base stations do not have adequate power backup. In the context of peer-to-peer streaming and TV applications, the system may turn to be non-dependable because simple attacks can ruin specific event streaming (e.g., popular broadcasts) which causes a higher-than-average amount of traffic; in these cases, simple traffic-volume based attacks can jeopardize the most useful (or prized) events.

Dependability is a security feature more critical for multicasting and broadcasting systems than for other systems because of the correlation between the value of the events and the number of peer/people wanting to receive them. Moreover, if the streamed event relates to critical public news, then the failure of the system represents not only a lack of security, but also a public/ social safety problem.

> *Node autonomy:* This is a system security goal that is somewhat specific to peer-to-peer systems. Each node is peer with all the others and its autonomous functioning should be guaranteed at all times: at any point during service, each node should be empowered to perform the actions that it is specified to perform at that step, without the need of external intervention. This does not mean that the node is isolated, nor that it cannot interact with other nodes or with external repositories, like in the ALTO IETF architecture [112], but that the node is not depending on this information for its operation. Dependencies on external intervention expose the node to trivial DoS attacks (when the information is not available, the node cannot work), and many other security threats. For instance, node autonomy is a requirement to prevent censorship attacks, and as discussed in the second example, the ability of de-correlating reboots or similar actions is fundamental to avoid massive failures that lead to information loss.

> *Access control:* Access control is fundamental to avoid frauds in commercial services, and fraud avoidance is a security goal. Access control can be a conflicting requirement with Node Autonomy. On the one hand,

to the best of our knowledge, there are no known methods for distributed authentication, so that, for this function, the node cannot be autonomous. On the other hand, it can be argued that a commercial system requires a form of centralized control (by the service provider) and is provided in exchange of some form of payment (direct or not). Thus in this case there is a commercial agreement between the two entities and any form, for instance, of denied access can be tracked and is not a DoS.

Access control is also a powerful means to reduce the possibility of security attacks coming from inside the system, because it prevents identity misrepresentation as well as, to some extent, collusion and multiple identities. The real challenge is providing access control while preserving the users privacy, i.e., implementing a system that either guarantees against information leakage (e.g., what TV channel is downloaded), or enables pseudonym-based authentication [119, 120].

2.13 DATA AND CONTENT SECURITY GOALS IN PEER-TO-PEER STREAMING

Considering now content management, there are some specific properties ofpeer-to-peer streaming that are of particular security interest:

- ➢ *Authenticity and integrity:* The data transmitted must be guaranteed and not tampered with, and it must be guaranteed that it was emitted by the intended transmission entity.
- ➢ *Non-repudiation:* Refers to the situation when the nodes that received a certain piece of data cannot deny that they received it. Non-repudiation is of interest only for video on demand applications, while for TV-like (broadcasting) it may be a minor feature.
- ➢ *Confidentiality:* The content that is transmitted during the streaming process can only be used or retransmitted to other nodes involved in the protocol. This property interlaces with access control. In fact an access control system that prevents unauthorized participation to a streaming, but is not supported by a content management system that can prevent recording and later replication of the content becomes useless. Recent studies on commercial TV streaming solutions have shown that they do not perform encryption [121], which makes the protocol lose not only confidentiality but also authenticity and integrity.
- ➢ *Anonymity:* This is one of the most controversial properties, since in many contexts the capability of a user to remain anonymous is associated to potentially unlawful activities. However, specifically in TV systems, the right of a user to watch a program without disclosing his identity is key to privacy protection and should be guaranteed by broadcasting systems. This property should be guaranteed also by peer-to-peer streaming systems, not only in face of external observers, but also with respect to the other users of the same system, and the broadcaster too.

Haridasan and van Renesse argue that not all applications need anonymity and confidentiality, but the features that matter most in frequent cases, are authenticity, integrity and non-repudiation [122]. Still, we have seen that anonymity becomes a key issue of privacy protection in TV systems. Non-repudiation, in the same systems, may be of secondary concern; unless a node can build claims on the fact that some information has not been delivered. Similarly to Section 2.9, these are clear differences of security requirements and other peer-to-peer applications.

2.14 PROTECTION MECHANISMS

As we have discussed, in peer-to-peer streaming there are two important values to be protected: i) the data exchanged between peers, and ii) the hardware and software resources that each user somehow 'lends' to the peer-to-peer system. In streaming systems the data being shared has a limited validity in time: after the target play out time the data turns stale. This adds a new dimension to the problem of data protection: delay makes data useless.

As a consequence, *bandwidth* becomes an asset that can be attacked to make data useless. As peer-to-peer systems are decentralized, it is usually easy for malicious peers to flood the system with junk and fake data in such a way that they would exhaust the bandwidth of the system [123].

Access control is a prevention mechanism that limits the reach of unwanted entities (peers) to the data being exchanged. Mapping and enforcing the connection between identities and access rights, access control strongly requires mechanisms for identity and reputation management. Some applications (e.g., public TV) require no access control for service provision, but others may be limited to groups of authorized users: membership is controlled, and the system should provide means to protect membership in face of attacks, both for breaking the control and for denying service to authorized members.

Auditing: Auditing is a detective means by which violations of predefined courses of actions can be identified. Unlike access control, auditing is an 'after the fact' measure and the outcome of its analysis influences future course of actions. Auditing requires the existence of logs with recordings of certain activity, the mechanism that is periodically triggered to write these logs, and an auditor—the entity verifying the logs. As far as the checking mechanism is involved, auditing can be continuous—at certain time intervals or on all records—or probabilistic—at random moments of time or on random recordings.

In peer-to-peer systems, audit can function as a means to check whether a peer node functions according to a predefined contract or protocol. The idea of distributed audit in the sense that nodes trade local storage with storage on other nodes is hinted in [117]. Of course, in order to perform it, the auditing method must be secured; this involves making sure that any nodes cannot influence what is being written in the logs, nor hide the logs themselves. Full access to query these logs must be entrusted to the requesting entity; moreover, the mechanism evaluating the events logged in the file must not misinterpret or ignore anything that was recorded. A simple way to ensure that most of these conditions are satisfied, is to impose a reward/punishment/incentive Mechanism that makes the entities involved in the audit process cheat as little as possible.

2.15 COMMON ATTACKS IN PEER-TO-PEER STREAMING SYSTEMS

The most serious attacks in peer-to-peer systems come from the inside of the system. This happens because only an internal node runs the protocols used between hosts, and can thus exploit them. It is common practice to restrict the set of actions that unknown nodes can perform. Once a node is allowed into the system, however, it is assumed to be honest hence it gets all privileges. With the problems presented, the bad nodes become bad on the fly. Therefore, the security of peer-to-peer application should look to protect internal nodes from other (malicious) internal nodes (Table 2.7). In what follows we will focus on some possible situations of vulnerability and describe the favorable conditions in which they take place. Each of the following attacks can exacerbate by *collusion*: one malicious entity compromises a (potentially large) collection of nodes to conduct correlated attacks onto the whole system. As expected, this is the most dangerous situation since it may be extremely difficult to track down the attacker if nodes function correctly at each step or on short-term, while overall misbehaving or deviating the protocol on the long run.

Table 2.7: Overview of attacks in peer-to-peer streaming systems

Attack	Target	Attribute
Forgery	data	confidentiality, integrity
Pollution	data	confidentiality, integrity
Eclipse	overlay, protocol	autonomy
Neighbor	protocol	autonomy

Attack	Target	Attribute
Sybil	protocol	authentication
DoS	peers	availability
Omission	peers, data	dependability

Forgery and Repudiation attacks: Forgery attacks break the condition of confidentiality and integrity of data mentioned in the previous section as a requirement of peer-to-peer streaming systems. Haridasan and van Renesse call *forgery* any fabricated or tampered data streamed into the system [118]. Repudiation attacks are attempts to deny having received streaming content or to acknowledge but with false information. Most cryptographic techniques as message signatures and public key infrastructures can easily solve the vulnerability, but suffers from the disadvantage that the performance cost of signatures or keys is high.

Pollution attacks in peer-to-peer streaming occur when the attacker mixes or substitutes junk pieces of data into the peer-to-peer distributed stream. In this way, the quality of the transmission decreases considerably: polluted chunks which arrive at fair peers degrade the stream quality and can change its meaning; and these peers will forward the *junk* to other peers and the whole effect will exponentially span over the network. Proof that the effects of this type of attack can be devastating in a streaming scenario are given by Dhungel et al., along with proposing four possible defenses: blacklisting, traffic encryption, hash verification and chunk signing [108].

Membership and Eclipse attacks: With this type of attacks, the membership protocol or the way nodes are admitted into the overlay are compromised. A special type of membership attack is the Eclipse attack, where, as noticed in [119], an attacker which controls a portion of the overlay neighbor scheme, *eclipses* fair nodes by dropping or re-routing any messages meant for those nodes. In other words, in Eclipse attacks, the attacker can gain some control over the routing mechanisms in thepeer-to-peer system.

Unstructured overlays are more susceptible to this type of attacks than the structured overlays; the latter do impose some constraints over the neighbors of one node, while the former do not. For this reason, the unstructured overlays use floods of random walks to gain knowledge of the network topology; the more they use these mechanisms, the higher the probability that an attacker will control more nodes in the system. One possible solution described in [119] is to use a mechanism that bounds the in-degree and out-degree of the nodes in the peer-to-peer overlay. In this way, an attacker is prevented from communicating with more nodes than those to which it normally should.

Neighbor selection attacks: These attacks refer to the situations in which an attacker controls the neighbor selection mechanism of some nodes, and makes them choose it as information provider. Malicious nodes can thus infiltrate and dominate sets of neighbors. The attacker will influence the way the overlay communicates and the neighbor selection process happens, so that it can control the traffic and subvert the whole system. These attacks are referred to as *epidemic* by [120], as fair nodes will "unknowingly reference compromised peers in their neighbor set." Of course, the problem is even worse if the membership server is itself attacked in this way. One idea of solving this problem with Distributed Hash Tables is to identify the invariants in the placement of peers in the overlay, and detect attacks in the form of deviations from these invariants. A solution adapted to mesh-based systems is shown in [120].

Sybil attacks: These attacks happen when the reputation mechanism established within the peer-to-peer system is compromised. Specifically, an attacker creates a large number of entities which bear the same disguised identity in order to become more powerful. Depending on how the id-s of nodes and reputation constraints are generated, the reputation system may be more or less vulnerable to such attacks. The idea is that once disguised the attacker profits from the trust that is given to the real entity it impersonates. Guarding against such attack may involve a trusted third entity which certifies that a name or a reputation id is attached to the exact entity it is supposed to carry it. Therefore, certified node identifier is one of the most straightforward techniques to repel masquerading. In addition to this method, auditing is another way to prevent the Sybil attack. An interesting solution employing auditing is provided in [119], where a node periodically challenges one of its neighbors to provide it with a list of that node's inbound contacts; if that list appears unfair or tampered with, then the requester node can act upon this discovery.

DoS attacks: Denial of Service can take many forms, from system partitioning to sending excessive amounts of requests or duplicate packets intended for their peers. The ability to bring a contribution to the streaming session is thus compromised, because a fair node would be flooded with useless messages or too many requests for it to handle. In this way, the resources of the system are exhausted with a relatively small effort on the attacker side. When the resource on which the attack focuses is bandwidth, the attack has been also termed as *request spreading attack* [117]. These problems were previously studied in the case of distributed systems as well as peer-to-peer streaming scenarios and there are several approaches in counteracting this type of attacks [117, 121, 122].

Omission attacks are at the other extreme than DoS attacks, implying that all the packet of data or just a part of it is not sent further according to the protocol specification. Again, just like for the DoS attacks, this behavior can compromise the whole peer-to-peer system even if a small number of peers collude. As noted by [123], the problem with this attack is that the guilt of a node cannot be proved easily.

2.16 CONCLUSION

There are two approaches to securing a peer-to-peer system: on the one hand, access control and identity management mechanisms can help to ensure that no malicious peers are allowed to join the system. This approach relies on the assumption that malicious behavior can be detected beforehand: peers refusing to comply with the rules of the protocol must not be accepted to join the system. On the other hand, peers can make promises they do not maintain afterwards. They can agree to be fair but eventually collude and unbalance the streaming process to their own advantage. In this second case, an audit-like mechanism can compensate the scheme. Observing what happens as the protocol is running can help an administrator determine if there are any system weak points that are being exploited. From this point of view, we think that a methodology is needed to detect that a peer-to-peer streaming system is under attack, and a study on what are the possible ways to compensate the damage. In streaming (as in any other) systems, attacks occur because there is a vulnerability to be exploited. Once an attack happens, it needs to be confined to an area of the peer-to-peer network as small as possible. Once the attacker cannot easily gain control over a bigger portion of the system, some mechanisms are needed to detect the target and source of the attack. It is not always easy to detect who the malicious nodes are (they are always from within the network, assuming that no other hosts can interfere with the protocol). There are some techniques that can be used for this purpose: one of them requires a trust manager [123], with the limitation that the machine needs to be replaced periodically, and should not be central to the whole network (since we want to eliminate single points of failures). A complementary approach is to use the mechanism of incentives and punishments, where nodes are stimulated to stick to the protocol; if they do not comply, then a distributed monitoring mechanism (performed via the malicious neighbors of a node) should help enforcing a punishment onto the bad performers. This incentive and punishment approach is so far the only distributed mechanism able to offer guarantees that on the long run, peer nodes will comply with the rules of the system.

REFERENCES

[1] Nicolas Christin, Andreas S. Weigend and John Chuang, Content Availability, "Pollution and Poisoning in Peer-to-Peer File Sharing Networks," Proceedings of the 6th ACM conference on Electronic commerce, 2005

[2] Ruichuan Chen, Eng Keong Lua, Jon Crowcroft, Wenjia Guo, Liyong Tang, Zhong Chen, "Securing Peer-to-Peer Content Sharing Service from Poisoning Attacks," Peer-to-Peer Computing, Eighth International Conference, 2008

[3] Stephanos Androutsellis-Theotokis and Diomidis Spinellis, "A Survey of Peer-to-Peer Content Distribution Technologies," ACM Computing Surveys, Vol. 36, No. 4, pp. 335–371, 2004

[4] Dan Boneh, Matthew Franklin, "Identity-Based Encryption from the Weil Pairing," SIAM J. of Computing, Vol. 32, No. 3, pp. 586–615, 2003.

[5] Lei Guo, Songqing Chen, Shansi Ren, Xin Chen, and Song Jiang, "PROP: a Scalable and Reliable P2P Assisted Proxy Streaming System," Distributed Computing Systems, 2004. Proceedings. 24th International Conference on 2004

[6] Ernesto Damiani, Sabrina De Capitani di Vimercati, Stefano Paraboschi, A ReputationBased Approach for Choosing Reliable Resources in PeertoPeer Networks, Proceedings of the 9th ACM conference on Computer and communications security ACM New York, NY, USA, 2002

[7] D. Dumitriu,_ E. Knightly,_ A. Kuzmanovic, _I. Stoica, and W. Zwaenepoel_,, DenialofService Resilience in PeertoPeer File Sharing Systems, Proceeding SIGMETRICS '05 Proceedings of the 2005 ACM SIGMETRICS international conference on Measurement and modeling of computer systems ACM New York, NY, USA, 2005.

[8] ToM Kalker, Dick Epema, Pieter Hartel, Inald Lagendijk, Maarten van Steen, Music2Share –Copyright-Compliant Music Sharing in P2P Systems, Proceedings of the IEEE, 2004.

[9] Balachander Krishnamurthy, Craig Wills, Yin Zhang, On the Use and Performance of ContentDistribution Networks, ACM Sigcomm Internet Measurement Workshop, 2001

[10] Stefan Saroiu, Krishna P. Gummadi, Richard J. Dunn, Steven D. Gribble, and Henry M. Levy, An Analysis of Internet Content Delivery Systems, ACM Sigcomm Internet Measurement Workshop, 2001

[11] Pablo Rodriguez, SeeMong Tan, Christos Gkantsidis, On the feasibility of Commercial, Legal P2P Content Distribution, ACM SIGCOMM Computer Communication Review Homepage archive Vol. 36 Issue. 1, 2006

[12] Matthew Yurkewych Brian N. Levine Arnold L. Rosenberg, On the Cost Ineffectiveness of Redundancy in Commercial P2P Computing, Proceeding CCS '05 Proceedings of the 12th ACM conference on Computer and communications security ACM New York, NY, USA,2005

[13] Runfang Zhou, Kai Hwang, GossipTrust for Fast Reputation Aggregation in Peer-to-Peer Networks, IEEE Transactions on Knowledgement and Data Engineering (TKDE-0003–0107R1, Finalized, 2008)

[14] T.Do, KA. Hua, and M. Tantaoui, "P2VoD: Providing Fault Tolerant Video-on-Demand Streaming in Peer-to-Peer Environment.," in the Proc. of the IEEE ICC, Paris, France, 20–24 Juin 2004

[15] X. Jiang, Y. Dong, D. Xu, and B. Bhargava, "GnuStream: a P2P Media Streaming System Prototype" IEEE International Conference on Multimedia and Expo Baltimore, MD, July 2003

[16] Duc A. Tran, Kien A. Hua, and Tai T. Do, "ZIGZAG: An Efficient Peer-to-Peer Scheme for Media Streaming.," In Proceedings of IEEE INFOCOM 2003, San Francisco, CA, USA, 30 Mars – 03 Avril 2003

[17] R. Rejaie, and A. Ortega, "PALS: Peer-to-Peer Adaptive Layered Streaming." in Proceedings of the International Workshop on Network and Operating Systems Support for Digital Audio and Video, Monterey, California, June 2003

[18] M. Hefeeda, A. Habib, B. Botev, D. Xu, and B. Bhargava, "PROMISE: Peer-to-Peer Media Streaming Using CollectCast.," In Proc. of ACM Multimedia 2003, pages 45--54, Berkeley, CA, Novembre 2003

[19] F. Pianese, J. Keller, and E. W. Biersack, "PULSE, a Flexible P2P Live Streaming System," in Proc. of 9th IEEE Global Internet Symposium Barcelona, Spain, 28 & 29 April 2006

[20] S. Traverso, E. Leonardi, M. Mellia, and M. Meo, "Network Awareness in P2P-TV Applications," 15th Open European Summer School and IFIP TC6.6 Workshop on The Internet of the Future, Barcelona, Spain, 2009

[21] H. Xie, A. Krishnamurthy, A. Silberschatz, and Y.Richard Yang, "P4P: Explicit Communications for Cooperative Control Between P2P and NetworkProviders," http://www.dcia.info/ documents/P4P_ Overview.pdf

[22] M. Eberhard, L. Celetto, C. Timmerer, E. Quacchio, H. Hellwagner, and F. Rovati, "An Interoperable Streaming Framework for Scalable Video Coding based on MPEG-21," Proceedings of the 5th IET Visual Information Engineering Conference Conference (VIE'08), Xi'an, China, July 2008

[23] http://www.ietf.org/html.charters/alto-charter.html

[24] http://www.rayv.com/cms/index.html

[25] http://www.peerialism.se/

[26] http://www.peeringportal.com/

[27] Y. Liu, X. Hei, C. Liang, and K. W. ROSS. "Insight into pplive: A measurement study of a largescale P2P iptv system" 2006

[28] T. Silverston and O. Fourmaux, "P2P iptv measurement: A comparison study.," http://www.arxiv.org/abs/ cs.NI/0610133, 2006.

[29] Jiehui JU, Fuwei FAN,, Jiyi WU, "Analysis of Model and Key Technology for P2P Network Route Security Evaluation with 2-tuple Linguistic Information," Journal of Computational Information Systems 9: 14, 2013

[30] Rahul J. Vaghela1, Kalpesh Patel," A Brief Comparison of Security Patterns for Peer to Peer Systems," IJAIEA, Vol.2, 2013

[31] Do-sik An, Byong-lae Ha and Gi-hwan Cho, "A Robust Trust Management Scheme against the Malicious Nodes in Distributed P2P Network," International Journal of Security and Its Applications Vol. 7, No. 3, May, 2013

[32] R.Geetha M.E, Nithya B.E, "Analysis of Streaming Services and Security Issues in Peer-to-Peer Network," IJCSNS International Journal of Computer Science and Network Security, VOL.13 No.4, 2013

[33] A. Suganya, P. Laura Juliet., "Enhancing Security and Response Time for Secure Search in Unstructured Peer to Peer Network," International Journal of Science and Research (IJSR), India Online ISSN: 2319-7064

[34] R.Suneelmanohar, T.V.Sai Krishna, "IRM: File Replication and Consistency Maintenance in P2P with security Maintenance through Routers," Research Journal of Computer Systems Engineering – RJCSE, Vol.03,2012

[35] Zied Trifa, Maher Khemakhem, "Taxonomy of Structured P2P Overlay Networks Security Attacks," World Academy of Science, Engineering and Technology 64, 2012

[36] Stephen S Kirkman, Kamyar Dezhgosha, "Security Review of P2P Applications and Networks,"

[37] Benjamin Schleinzer, Nobukazu Yoshioka, "A Security Pattern for Data Integrity in P2P Systems" Cite Seer

[38] Tien Tuan Anh Dinh and Mark Ryan, "Checking Security Property of P2P Systems Using CSP"

[39] Michele Amoretti, "A Survey of Peer-to-Peer Overlay Schemes: Effectiveness, Efficiency and Security," Recent Patents on Computer Science 2009

[40] Markus Fiedler, Charlott Eliasson, Tomasz Ciszkowski, Wojciech Mazurczyk and Zbigniew Kotulski, "Parameterisation of a reputation system for VoIP in P2P networks for improved communication quality and security, BTH/EuroFGI, 2008

[41] Miguel Castro, Peter Druschel, Ayalvadi Ganesh, Antony Rowstron and Dan S. Wallach, "Secure routing for structured peer-to-peer overlay networks," Citeseer, 2002

[42] Nithya.M.R, Geetha.R. "Analysis of Streaming Services and Security" Issues in Peer-To-Peer Network, IJCSET, 2012

[43] Mokhtarian.K and Hefeeda.M. "Capacity Management of Seed Servers in Peer-to-Peer Streaming Systems with Scalable Video Streams," IEEE, 2012.

[44] Singh.A.K, Maheshwari.S, Verma.S and Dekar.R, "Peer to Peer Secure Communication in Mobile Environment: A Novel Approach," International Journal of Computer Applications, pp-0975 – 8887, vol 52– No.9, August 2012.

[45] Sudhan.K.S, Thangaraj.P, DeepaPrabha.G, "Achieving Quality of Metric for Video Streaming Service in the Warehouse Application with Coexisting of IEEE 802.11 a/b/g Standards," International Journal of Computer Applications,2012.

[46] Esteves.A.F.F.E "Detection of Encrypted Traffic Generated by Peer-to-Peer Live Streaming Applications Using Deep Packet Inspection," 2011.

[47] Dittrich.H, "Analyzing the Security of Incentive Schemes in P2P-based File-sharing Systems," 2012

[48] Araujo.R.D,Ferreira.H.N.M, Rosa.P.F, Gonc.R, Cattelan.A. "A Redundancy Information Protocol for P2P Networks in Ubiquitous Computing Environments: Design and Implementation," International Conference on Networks, 2012.

[49] Kumar.P.P, Naini.K Reddy.S, Krishna.R.S, Kumar.K, Ramesh.M,"Preventive Measures For Malware In P2P Networks," International Journal of Engineering Research and Applications (IJERA), 2012

[50] Liu.J, Zhang.L, Fan.S-H, Guo.C, He.S, and Chang.G.K, "A novel architecture for peer-to-peer interconnect in millimeter-wave radio-over- fiber access networks," Progress In Electromagnetics Research, Vol. pp.126, 139–148, 2012.

[51] Carra D, Lo Cigno R, Biersack EW, "Graph based analysis of mesh overlay streaming systems," IEEE J Sel Areas Commun, Vol. 25, pp.1667–1677, 2007

[52] Carra D, Lo Cigno R, Biersack EW, "Stochastic graph processes for performance evaluation of content delivery applications in overlay networks," IEEE Trans Parallel Distrib Syst 19:247–261, 2008

[53] Jelasity M, Montresor A, Babaoglu O, "T-Man: gossipbased fast overlay topology construction," Elsevier Comput Networks 53:2321–2339, 2009

[54] Liu Y, Guo Y, Liang C, "A survey on peer-to-peer video streaming systems," Peer-to-Peer Networking and Applications, Vol. 1(1), pp.18–28, 2008

[55] Magharei N, Rejaie R, Guo Y, "Mesh or multiple-tree: a comparative study of live P2P streaming approaches," In: Proc of the 26th IEEE int conference on computer communications (INFOCOM'07), pp 1424–1432, 2007

[56] Seibert J, Zage D, Nita-Rotaru C, "Won't you be my neighbor? Neighbor selection attacks in meshbased peer-topeer streaming" Technical Report, Purdue University, 2008

[57] Zhou M, Liu J, "Ahybrid overlay network for video-ondemand," In: Proc of the IEEE int conference on communications (ICC'08), pp 1309–1311, 2005

[58] Kermarrec A-M, van Steen M, "Gossiping in distributed systems," SIGOPS Oper Syst Rev 41(5):pp2–7, 2007

[59] Shetty S, Galdames P, Tavanapong W, Cai Y, "Detecting malicious peers in overlay multicast streaming," In: Proc of the 31st IEEE conference on local computer networks (LCN'06), Florida, 2006

[60] Magharei N, Rejaie R, "PRIME: peer-to-peer receiverdriven mesh-based streaming," In: Proc of the 26th IEEE int conference on computer communications (INFOCOM'07). IEEE, pp 1415–1423, 2007

[61] Zhang X, Liu J, Li B, Yum Y-S, "CoolStreaming/ DONet: a data-driven overlay network for peer-to-peer live media streaming," In: Proc of the 24th IEEE int conference on computer communications (INFOCOM'05), vol 3, pp 2102–2111, 2005

[62] Muller, W., Eisenhardt, M., Henrich, A., "Efficient content-based P2P image retrieval using peer content descriptions," SPIE Electronic Imaging, 2004

[63] Jung, E.H., Cho, S.Y., "A Robust Digital Watermarking System Adopting 2D Barcode against Digital Piracy on P2P network," International Journal of Computer Science and Network Security, Vol.6, No.10, 2006

[64] Chu, C.C, Su, X., Prabhu, B.S., Gadh, R., Kurup, S., Sridhar, G., Sridhar, V., "Mobile DRM for Multimedia Content Commerce in P2P Networks," IEEE, 2006

[65] Kumar, S., Sivaprakasam, P., "A New Approach for Encrypting and Decrypting Data in Images among users in Ad hoc Network," European Journal of Scientific Research, Vol. 92, No 3, pp.425–430, 2012

[66] Mathieu, B., Guelvouit, G.L., Desoubeaux, M., "Mitigating illegal contents via watermarking in video streaming P2P network," Proceedings of IEEE Advanced Networks and Telecommunication Systems, 2010

[67] Meddour, D.E., Mushtaq, M., Ahmed, T., "Open Issues in P2P Multimedia Streaming," MULTICOMM, 2006

[68] Berson, T., "Skype security evaluation," Anagram Laboratories, 2005

[69] Tang, Y., Luo, J.G., Zhang, Q., Zhang, M., and Yang, S-H, "Deploying P2P Networks for Large-Scale Live Video-Streaming Service," IEEE Communications Magazine, 2007

[70] Hughes, D., Walkerdine, J., "Distributed video encoding over a peer-to-peer network," PREP, 2005

[71] Reforgiato, D., Lombardo, A., Schembra, G., "A P2P Platform based on Rate-Controlled FGS encoding for Broadcast Video Transmission to Heterogeneous Terminals with Heterogeneous Network Access," GTTI, 2009

[72] Hagemeister, P., "Censorship-resistant Collaboration with a Hybrid DTN/P2P Network," Masters Thesis, 2012

[73] Ha, I., Wildman, S. S., & Bauer, J. M. "P2P, CDNs, and hybrid networks: The economics of Internet video Distribution," International Telecommunications Policy Review, Vol. 17(4),pp. 1–22, 2010

[74] Saisaranya, T., & Kalaivani, R. "A Scheme to support P2P-Based Multimedia Sharing in Multimedia Board," 2013

[75] Mottalib, M. A., Md Ali Al Mamun, M., Ehsannuzaman, R. H., & Kaysar, J. "A Combined Approach of Reputation Based Defense Mechanism in P2P Live Video Streaming," 2013

[76] Ozturk. M and Clincy. V, "Understanding the effect of network-coding and video-encoding on multimedia streaming for peer-to-peer (P2P) systems in wireless networks,"2012

[77] Almeida,R.B.D., Vieira A.B., Paula.A., Silva,C, "An´alise do Impacto de Ataques de Poluiç̃ao Combinado com Whitewashing em Sistemas P2P de Live Streaming," 2012

[78] Anandaraj, M., Ganeshkumar, P., & Vijayakumar, K. P, "An Efficient QOS Based Multimedia Content Distribution Mechanism in P2P Network," International Journal, 3(5), 2013

[79] Chu, C. C., Su, X., Prabhu, B. S., Gadh, R., Kurup, S., Sridhar, G., & Sridhar, V, "Mobile DRM for multimedia content commerce in P2P networks," In IEEE consumer communications and networking conference, 2006

[80] Pakstas, A., Wang, F., Mikusauskas, R., Yang, W, "VoDPStream- the Optimized Design and Implementation of a P2P-based VoD System," 2012

[81] Mathieu, B.,Le Guelvouit, G., Desoubeaux, M, "Mitigating illegal contents via watermarking in video streaming P2P network," 2010

[82] Lin, W. S., Zhao, H. V., & Liu, K. R. "Cooperation Stimulation Strategies for Peer-To-Peer Wireless Video Streaming Social Networks," Image Processing, IEEE Transactions, Vol. 19(7), pp. 1768–1784, 2010

[83] Neysiani, B. S., Neematbakhsh, N., Barekatain, B., Maarof, M. A., Zamanifar, K,"Understanding Pull-based Method Efficiency in Peer-to-Peer Live Video Streaming over Mesh Networks," 2012

[84] Aguirre Pastor, J. V., Álvarez Sánchez, R. I., Tortosa Grau, L., & Vicent Francés, J. F., "Incorporating global positioning data in real time P2P audio/video streams for mobile devices," 2008

[85] Favalli, L., Folli, M., Lombardo, A., Reforgiato, D., Schembra, G. "A P2P platform for real-time multicast video streaming leveraging on scalable multiple descriptions to cope with bandwidth fluctuations," International Journal of Computer Networks and Communications (IJCNC). Vol.6, 2011

[86] Trifa, Z., & Khemakhem, M. "Taxonomy of Structured P2P Overlay Networks Security Attacks," In Proceedings of World Academy of Science, Engineering and Technology (No. 64). World Academy of Science, Engineering and Technology, 2012

[87] William Conner, Klara Nahrstedt, Indranil Gupta "Preventing DoS Attacks in Peer-to-Peer Media Streaming Systems" Computer Science, Vol. 5060/2008, 13–20, DOI: 10.1007/978-3-540-69295-9_3, 2008

[88] Ratan Guha Darshan Purandare "Security Issues in BitTorrent like P2P Streaming Systems" Society for Computer Simulation VOL 38; PART 4, pp. 423–430. 2006

[89] Maya Haridasan and Robbert van Renesse "SecureStream: An Intrusion-Tolerant Protocol for Live-Streaming Dissemination" Computer Communications, Vol. 31, Nr. 3, 563–575, 2007

[90] William Conner and Klara Nahrstedt "Securing Peer-to-Peer Media Streaming Systems from Selfish and Malicious Behavior" IEEE International Conference on November Page(s): 899–902, 2007

[91] Xiaoyun Liu, Tiejun Huang, Longshe Huo, Luntian Mou "A DRM architecture for manageable P2P based iptv system"

[92] Hao Yin, Chuang Lin, Qian Zhang, Zhijia Chen, and Dapeng Wu "TrustStream: A Secure and Scalable Architecture for Large-Scale Internet Media Streaming" IEEE Transactions On Circuits And Systems For Video Technology, VOL. 18, NO. 12, 2008

[93] W. Sabrina Lin, H. Vicky Zhao and K. J. Ray Liu "Attack-resistant cooperation strategies in P2P live streaming social Networks" Systems and Computers, 1373–1377 42nd Asilomar Conference, 2008

[94] Jan Seedorf "Security Issues for P2P-based Voice- and Video-Streaming Applications" Information and communication technology, Vol.309/2009, 95–110, DOI: 10.1007/978-3-642-05437-2_10, 2009

[95] Bertrand Mathieu, Pierre Paris, Soufiane Rouibia "A Secure and Legal Network-aware P2P VoD System" Internet and Web Applications and Services (ICIW), 2010 Fifth International Conference, Vol.9–15, 2010

[96] Mikko Uitto and Janne Vehkaperä "Video Quality Assurance for SVC in Peer-to-Peer Streaming" AP2PS: The Third International Conference on Advances in P2P Systems, 2011

[97] Ahmed Hamza and Adrian Kwok "A primer on video streaming over peer-to-peer networks" International Conference on Multimedia and Expo, pages 1417–1420, December 2nd 2010

[98] Istemi EkinAkkusa, Öznur Özkasap, M.RehaCivanlar "Peer-to-peer multipoint video conferencing with layered video" Journal of Network and Computer Applications, Vol. 34, pp. 137–150, 2011

[99] Hareesh.K and Manjaiah D.H "Peer-to-peer live streaming and video on demand design issues and its challenges" International Journal of Peer to Peer Networks (IJP2P) Vol.2, No.4, 2011

[100] Tsao-TaWei, Chia-HuiWang, Yu-Hsien Chu, and Ray-I Chang "A Secure and StableMulticast Overlay Network with Load Balancing for Scalable IPTV Services" International Journal of Digital Multimedia Broadcasting Article ID 540801, 12 pages doi:10.1155/2012/540801, 2012

[101] Gabriela Gheorghe, Renato Lo Cigno, Alberto Montresor, "Security and Privacy Issues in P2P Streaming Systems: A Survey," Technical Report TR-DISI-09-001,Version: 1.0, August 17, 2009

[102] Dhungel P, Hei X, Ross KW, Saxena N, "The pollution attack in P2P live video streaming: measurement results and defenses," In: Proc of the 2007 workshop on peer-topeer streaming and IP-TV (P2P-TV'07). ACM, New York, pp 323–328, 2007

[103] Yang S, Jin H, Li B, Liao X, "A modeling framework of content pollution in Peer-to-Peer video streaming systems," Comput Networks, Vol. 53(15):2703–2715, 2009

[104] Singh K, Schulzrinne H, "Peer-to-peer internet telephony using SIP. In: Proc of the int workshop on network and operating systems support for digital audio and video (NOSSDAV'05)," ACM, Stevenson, pp 63–68, 2005

[105] Jennings C, Lowekamp B, Rescorla E, Baset S, Schulzrinne H, "REsource LOcation And Discovery (RELOAD) v. 6, P2PSIP Internet-Draft," IETF. *http://tools.ietf.org/html/* draft-ietf-P2Psip-base-06. Accessed 9 Nov 2009

[106] Dabek F et al "Building Peer-to-Peer Systems with Chord, a Distributed Lookup Service," In: Proc of the 8th workshop, 2001

[107] Rowstron A, Druschel P, "Pastry: scalable, decentralized object location and routing for large-scale peer-to-peer systems," In: Proc of the 18th int conf on distributed Systems Platforms, Heidelberg, 2001

[108] Slashdot "Skype blames Microsoft patch Tuesday for outage," http://slashdot.org/articles/07/08/20/150258.shtml, 2007

[109] Liu Y, Guo Y, Liang C "A survey on peer-to-peer video streaming systems. Peer-to-Peer Networking and Applications," Vol.1(1), pp.18–28. http://www.springerlink.com/content/ c62114g6g4863t32, 2008

[110] Leonardi E, Mellia M, Horvath A, Muscariello L, Niccolini S, Rossi D, "Building a cooperative P2P-TV application over a wise network: the approach of the European FP-7 strep NAPA-WINE," IEEE Commun Mag, Vol.46(4), pp.20–22, 2008

[111] Wallach DS, "A survey of peer-to-peer security issues. In: Okada M, Pierce BC, Scedrov A, Tokuda H, Yonezawa A (eds) Proc of the Mext-NSF-JSPS int symposium on software security—theories and systems (ISSS'02), LNCS, vol 2609. Springer, Tokyo, pp 42–57, 2003

[112] Seedorf J, Burger E, "Application-layer traffic optimization (ALTO) problem statement. RFC 5693, IETF, 2009

[113] Bianchi G, Bonola M, Falletta V, Proto FS, Teofili S, "The sparta pseudonym and authorization system," Sci Comput Program Vol. 74(1–2), pp. 23–33, 2008

[114] Camenisch J, Lysyanskaya A, "An efficient system for non-transferable anonymous credentials with optional anonymity revocation," In: Proc of the int conference on the theory and application of cryptographic techniques (EUROCRYPT '01). London, UK, Springer-Verlag, pp 93–118, 2001

[115] Ciullo D, Mellia M, Meo M, Leonardi E, "Understanding P2P-TV systems through real measurements," In: Proc of the IEEE global telecommunications conference (GLOBECOM'08, 2008

[116] Haridasan M, van Renesse R, "SecureStream: an intrusion-tolerant protocol for live-streaming dissemination," Comput Commun, Vol.31(3), pp. 563–575, 2008

[117] Conner W, Nahrstedt K, "Securing peer-to-peer media streaming systems from selfish and malicious behavior," In: MDS'07: Proc of the 4th on Middleware doctoral symposium. ACM, New York, pp 1–6, 2007

[118] Haridasan M, van Renesse R, "Defense against intrusion in a live streaming multicast system," In: Proc of the 6th IEEE int conference on peer-to-peer computing (P2P'06). IEEE Computer Society, Cambridge, pp 185–192, 2006

[119] Singh A, Castro M, Druschel P, Rowstron A, "Defending against eclipse attacks on overlay networks," In: Proc of the 11th workshop on ACM SIGOPS European workshop, p 21, 2004

[120] Seibert J, Zage D, Nita-Rotaru C, "Won't you be my neighbor? Neighbor selection attacks in mesh-based peer-topeer streaming," Technical Report, Purdue University, 2008

[121] Conner W, Nahrstedt K, Gupta I, "Preventing DoS attacks in peer-to-peer media streaming systems," In: Proc of the 13th annual conference on multimedia computing and networking (MMCN'06), San Jose, 2006

[122] Yang J, Li Y, Huang B, Ming J, "Preventing DDoS attacks based on credit model for P2P streaming system," In: ATC '08: Proc of the 5th international conference on autonomic and trusted computing. Springer, Berlin, pp 13–20, 2008

[123] Shetty S, Galdames P, Tavanapong W, Cai Y, "Detecting malicious peers in overlay multicast streaming," In: Proc of the 31st IEEE conference on local computer networks (LCN'06), Florida, 2006

chapter 3

FRAMEWORK FOR MITIGATING ILLEGITIMATE PEER

3.1 OVERVIEW

The chapter of this book offers a framework for providing countermeasures against the illegal peer nodes in the network. The objective of framework is to identify unauthenticated nodes in the network, monitor their joining request, and implements important security mechanism to preserve the confidential data against unauthorized act by an attacker in peer-to-peer network. The peer-to-peer multimedia-sharing network is recent trend in delivering large amount of file to enormous number of participants. The unauthenticated users are punished by means of poisoning the network, which raises immense legal issues in the field of P2P network. The prominent reason of the illegitimate multimedia file sharing are found as peer nodes which overlook the various rights as well as attempt to mitigate the various illegitimate peer nodes. Conventional content delivery networks will use a huge quantity of the proxy digital content servers spread over globally distributed WANs. The content distributors need to replicate or cache contents on many servers. The bandwidth demand and resources needed to maintain these CDNs are very expensive. A P2P content network significantly reduces the distribution cost, since many content servers are eliminated and open networks are used. P2P networks improve the content availability, as any peer can serve as a content provider. P2P networks are desired to be scalable, because more peers or providers lead to faster content delivery.

The legitimate clients are considered as the entity in the network which obeys the digital rights management and other restrictions. Pirates are peers attempting to download some content file without paying or authorization. The colluders are those paid clients who share the contents with pirates. We use identity-based signatures (IBS) to secure file indices. IBS offers the same level of security as PKI-based signatures with much less overhead. We apply discriminatory content poisoning against pirates. We focus on protection of decentralized P2P content networks. Protecting centralized P2P networks like Napster or mp3.com is much simpler than the schemepresented in this chapter. So, the goal is to stop collusive piracy within the boundary of a P2P content delivery network. The protection scheme works nicely in a P2P network environment. The scheme cannot stop randomized piracy in open Internet using Email attachment or any other means to spread copyrighted contents, illegally. Randomized piracy is beyond the scope of this study.

3.2 ANALYTICAL FOUNDATION FOR MITIGATING ILLEGAL PEER

In this section, we provide a detailed overview of the framework with objective to design such a protocol that should consist of reduced delivery cost, maximized digital content availability and copyright compliance while exploring P2P network resources. The designed model should also be sufficiently effective and enough to mitigate the collusive piracy within the peer to peer content delivery network. The following are the main focus area of the framework which is as given below:

➤ Error-free identification of colluders and pirates.

➤ Creation of secure protocol for forwarding poisoned chunk of data to illegitimate client in network.

➤ Creation of protocol for preventing colluders to come in contact with legitimate clients in the network.

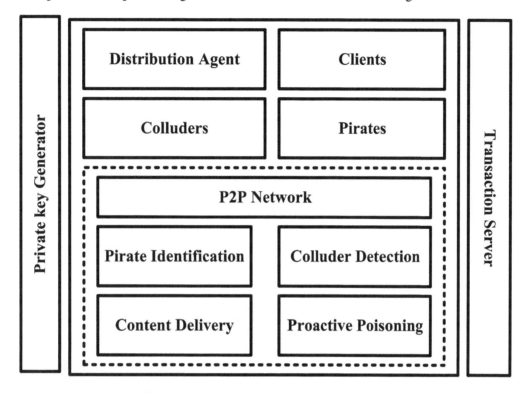

Figure 3.1: Architecture of the proposed model

Fig. 3.1 shows the overall architecture of the proposed "proactive content poisoning" system where the main components will be Distribution agent, Clients, Colluders, and Pirates. The next phase of architecture will consist of identifying the pirates and colluders, content delivery, and proactive poisoning. The technique used will be to initiate a design of methodology for authenticating peer with IP address and definitely port number. These entities will evaluate the component peers when the download or the upload of the digital content takes place where each of the peers will attempt to identify the illegitimate peers. The work carried through the proposed framework will seek authentication for the peer looking to download or upload the file and in case the authentication fails for showing existence of illegitimate client in the network, the proposed system model will direct poisoned chunks to the illegitimate peer. The proposed technique can be suitably used in order to identify colluders. The flow of the proposed model is shown in Fig. 3.2.

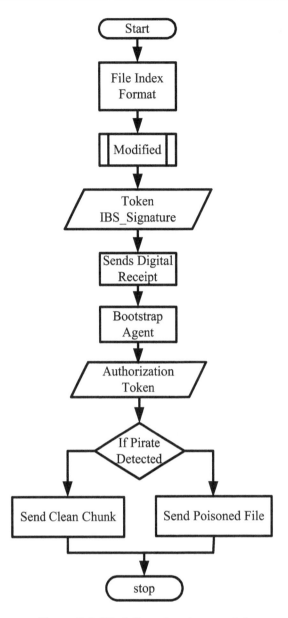

Figure 3.2: Work flow of system model

The above Fig. 3.2 shows the pro process flow diagram for the proposed system model of proactive content poisoning. The proposed technique uses the concept of forwarding poisoned chunks to discourage the illegitimate peer existing in the P2P network, where the restricted poison identification potential is exploited and enforce the pirate to reject the clean chunks downloaded along with the poisoned chunks. Creation of such technique will induce the highly increased download time for the unauthorized client thereby discourage their interest and allow secure transmission to the service provider to legitimate client. The goal of work effort is achieved with robustness parameters like download time, processing time, encryption and decryption time, packet delivery ratio, unauthorized peer request, inter packet delay and bandwidth consumption.

3.3 THE CORE METHODOLOGY OF THE PROPOSED FOUNDATION

The part of the study incorporates different design aspects of empirical and experimental-based methodology by deploying identity-based signature in order to secure the file indexes. The theoretical analysis of method is used for the proposed study provides equivalent standards of security as PKI-based signatures along with much reduced control overhead. The simulation work is carried out using Matlab by applying discriminatory content poisoning against pirate nodes by concentrating on the security of the decentralized P2P content networks. The prime basis of the adopted methodology is to ensure that data packet transmitted in P2P network very safely; however, controlling the malicious node is never possible by any security programs optimally. Hence, the proposed system ensures that even if the data packet falls in the captivity of the malicious node, than their (malicious node) interest is never met. This is done by forwarding the poisoned data to the malicious node, which is known as pirates. Content poisoning is often treated as a security threat to P2P Networks. We make the following specific contributions towards P2P content delivery.

> **Distributed Detection of Colluders and Pirates**: We develop a protocol that identifies a peer with its endpoint address. File index format is changed to incorporate a digital signature based on this identity. A peer authentication protocol is developed to establish the legitimacy of a peer when it downloads and uploads the file. Using IBS, the system enables each peer to identify unauthorized peers or pirates without the need for communication with a central authority.

> **Proactive Content Poisoning of Detected Pirates**: The protocol requires sending poisoned chunks to any detected pirate requesting a protected file. If all clients simply deny download request without poisoning, the pirates can still accumulate clean chunks from colluders that are willing to share. With poisoning, pirates are forced to discard even clean chunks received. This will prolong their download time to a level beyond practical limit. Experiments show that it is unlikely that a pirate can download a clean copy of the file.

> **Containment of Peer Collusion to Stage Piracy**: The system is unique from any existing P2P copyright protection scheme in that we recognize that peer collusion is inevitable: a paid customer may intentionally collude with pirates; a pirate may also hack into client hosts and turn them into unwilling colluders. The system is designed so that even with large number of colluders, a pirate will still suffer from intolerably long download time. We also present a random collusion detection mechanism to further enhance the system.

> **Trusted P2P Platform for Copyrighted Content Delivery**: Hardware investment for P2P content delivery is much lower than that required in any existing CDNs. The system only uses a few distribution agents to serve large number of clients. The system is highly scalable, robust to peer and link failures, and easily deployed in Gnutella, KaZaA, eMule networks, etc. All claimed advantages are backed by performance analysis and simulation results.

The proposed system is designed with 4 categories of peer as:

> **Clients**: This type of the peer are normally the authorized peer within the network.
> **Colluders**: This type of the peers are paid peers who are sharing contents with other legitimate peers.
> **Distribution agents**: These are the set of trusted peers which are controlled by the digital content owners for file distribution.
> **Pirates**: These are unpaid or unauthorized clients who are always at lookout of some unauthorized downloads of premium contents.

The proposed design also includes a transaction server (see Fig. 3.1) which is assumed to be managing the buying and billing related issues. The transaction server will receive the request from the clients in the network. The communications among the peers are secured by configuring a private key generator in order to generate set of private keys with Identity-Based Signatures (IBS).

The private key generator also acts as certificate authority in various secure communications. When the peers will attempt to get themselves connected in a network, the system will deploy the key generator and transaction server.

Along with invocation of IBS, the peer communication will not be depended on any public key specially designed as their identity itself will serve as the key of public type.

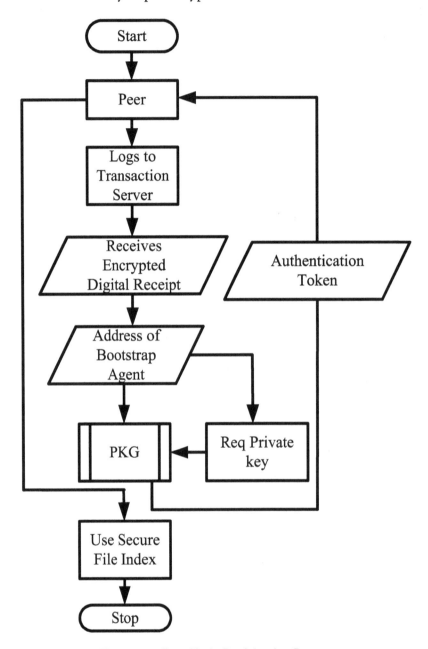

Figure 3.3: Peer Node Participation Process

The system model will initiate with colluders, paid clients, as well as pirate without indexing for their identification. The proposed prototype system model is designed to quantize them involuntarily. The model also consists of a bootstrap unit as an input point of entry which is chosen from one of the distribution agent. The existing network designs involuntarily declare its identification without any type of identification. In order to deal with this, the system model uses port number and IP address instead to any other types of authentication parameters that can be possible used in the same set of the network. A complete connection with the peer is only ensured when it is reachable via any listening port on its host.

The above Fig. 3.3 shows process flow diagram for peer participating process where it can be understood that each legitimate peer has a valid token (use indication). The token (indication) will be have possession of validity for a very minimized instant of time in order for the peer components to update in constant time duration. The file-index format is modified in order to include a token (indication) and signature, which will be used by the peer nodes for securing the download permission. The system model will use the identification of the listening port as valid identification of the peer. The model also assumes that every peer node posses a better configured listening ports.

It was also found that the majority of the peer to peer clients will linked themselves to the World Wide Web using their home network where the fundamental standard will be to deploy network address translation equipment for sending forward incoming ports. The issue surfaces when a large quantity of the peer is behind a single network address translation are used. The public key to be used in the peer's end will be considered as end point address for which there is absolutely no requirement of encoding the contents of the file thereby minimizing the feasibility of network overhead. The model deploys the bootstrap unit in order to forward the incoming request. The client module will be not disclosed about the identity of the all units apart from bootstrap unit, which prevents the malicious peer node to blacklist or initiate an attack on the distribution agent.

The implementation of the work is carried out in 32 bit windows OS of 1.8 GHz with dual core processor. The programming is carried out in java platform. Although it is a very tough assignment to perform this experiment for real-time peer to peer network for evaluating the copyright infringement. The proposed simulation work is carried out in three phases:

➤ Estimation of the chunk poisoning rate.
➤ Estimation of the download time.
➤ Comparative analysis of resistance and overhead in fortification information gather.

The simulation environment of the proposed system is as shown below in Fig. 3.4.

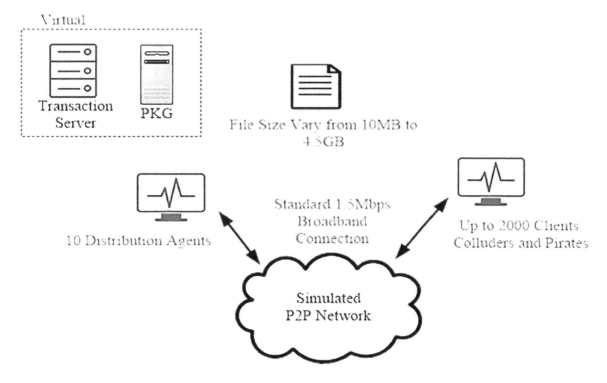

Figure 3.4: Simulation Scenario considered

The proposed framework will perform in three levels again:

> ➢ The top level will work towards emulating the peer to peer transmission.
> ➢ The intermediate level will be used for emulating the patterns of the considered peer types (distribution agents, legitimate clients, colluders, illegal pirates.)
> ➢ The bottom level will be allocated for data aggregation and information updating.

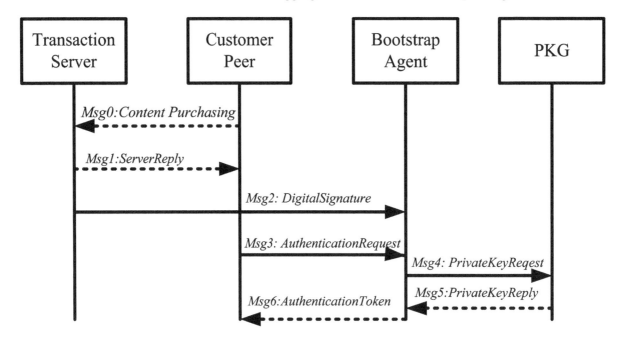

Figure 3.5: Sequence diagram of the simulation considered

As shown in Fig. 3.5.the simulation is conducted in the same procedure. When a peer node will participate in the network, it has to initially access the transaction server in order to complete the payment process for possessing the digital content. Once the transaction is completed, a digital acceptance slip consisting of the basic information of the content and identification of the clients will be in possession of the client. This digital acceptance slip will be lock in such a procedure that only the legitimate owner of the digital content will be able to unlock it. The address of bootstrap unit is possessed by the authorized client. The newly created digital acceptance slip will be considered for authenticating the newly participating client with bootstrap unit. As the bootstrap unit is configured by the actual owner of the digital content, therefore it unlocks the acceptance slip and authenticates its verification parameters. The transaction server will assign a session key for securing the privacy in the communication channel. Design of a legitimate token takes place when the bootstrap unit request key from the key generator. The existences of the pirates are scrutinized by the peers by evaluating the legitimacy of the supplementary signatures in the index of the files. This scheme of security is deployed by the legitimate peer nodes to distribute clean digital (Fig. 3.6).

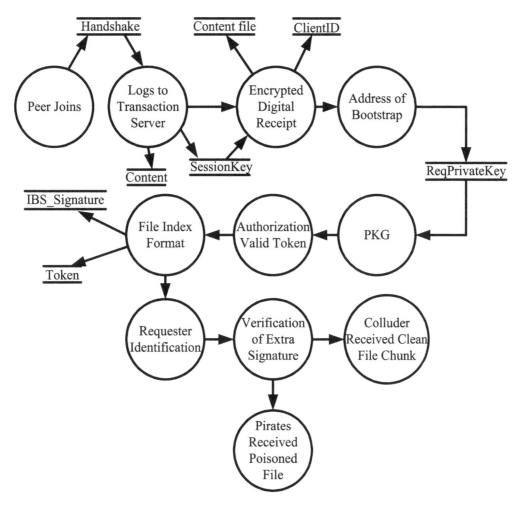

Figure 3.6: Data Flow Diagram of the proposed model

Contents explicitly among the peer nodes and use the forwarding of the digital content poisoning procedure to the unauthorized clients in peer to peer network. The considered tokens which are time-stamped makes sure that identified colluders should not be able to posses newly generated token once the old token perishes.

In a P2P content distribution network, only the content owner can verify the user ID/password pair; peers cannot check each other's identity. Revealing a user's identity to other peers violates his or her privacy. To solve this problem, we developed a PAP protocol. First, we apply IBS to secure file indexing. Then we outline the procedure to generate tokens. Finally, we specify the PAP protocol that authorizes file access to download by peers.

3.3.1 Secure File Indexing

In a P2P file-sharing network, a file index is used to map a file ID to a peer endpoint address. When a peer requests to download a file, it first queries the indexes that match a given file ID. Then the requester downloads from selected peers pointed by the indexes. To detect pirates from paid clients, we propose to modify file index to include three interlocking components: an authorization token, a timestamp, and a peer signature.

Each legitimate client has a valid token assigned by its bootstrap agent. The timestamp indicates the time when a token expires. Thus, the peer needs to refresh the token periodically. This short-lived token is designed for protecting copyright against colluders. The cost at each distribution agent to refresh the client tokens is rather limited, as shown via experiments. The peer signature is signed with the private key generated by PKG. This signature proves the authenticity of a peer.Download requests make explicit references to file indexes. The combined effects of the three extra fields ensure that all references to the file indexes are secured. Peers identify the pirates by checking the validity of the token and the signature in a file index. These features secure the P2P network operations to safeguard the sharing of clean contents among the paid clients.

3.3.2 File-Level Token Generation

First, both the transaction server and the PKG are fully trusted. Their public keys are known to all peers. The PAP protocol consists of two integral parts: token generation and authorization verification. When a peer joins the P2P network, it first sends authorization request to the bootstrap agent. All messages between a peer and its bootstrap agent are encrypted using the session key assigned by the transaction server at purchase time. A token is a digital signature of a three tuple: {peer endpoint, file ID, timestamp} signed by the private key of the content owner. Since bootstrap agent has a copy of the digital receipt sent by transaction server, verifying the receipt is thus done locally. The Decript (Receipt) function decrypts the digital receipt to identify the file λ. The Observe (requestor) returns with the endpoint address p. The Owner Sign (λ, p, t_s) function returns with a token.Upon receiving a private key, the bootstrap agent digitally signs the file ID, endpoint address, and timestamp to create the token. The reply message contains a four tuple: {endpoint address, peer private key, timestamp, token}. The reply message from bootstrap agent is encrypted usingthe assigned session key. The cost at each distribution agent to refresh the tokens is rather limited. In the experiments, there are 10 distribution agents to serve 1,000 clients/colluders. Each token refresh requires transmitting at most 2 KB of data and each peer is required to refresh its token in every 10 minutes. Per each agent, there are 1; 000 = 10 ¼ 100 peers refreshing tokens in10 minutes, Hence, we need to transmit only 100 x 2 KB ¼ 200 KB to refresh the tokens in every 10 minutes. Considering a standard broadband link capacity of 1.5 Mbps bandwidth, such a low refreshing overhead is negligible.

3.3.3 The Peer Authorization Protocol

The PAP protocol is formally specified below. A client must verify the download privilege of a requesting peer before clean file chunks are shared with the requestor. If the requestor fails to present proper credentials, the client must send poisoned chunks, as shown in Fig. 3.7.

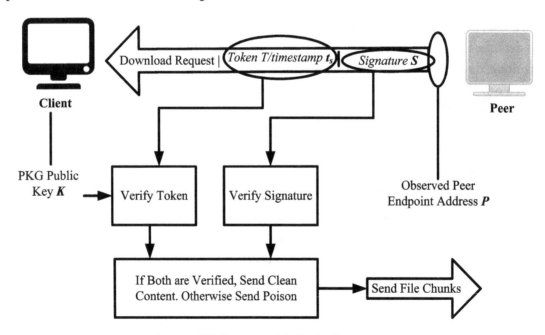

Figure 3.7: Schema of Authorization protocol

In PAP, a download request applies a token T, file index Φ, timestamp t_s, and the peer signature S. If any of the fields are missing, the download is stopped. A download client must have a valid token T and signature S. Two pieces of critical information are needed: public key K of PKG and the peer endpoint address p. The protocol verifies both token T and signature S. File index Φ (λ, p) contains the peer endpoint address p and the file ID λ. Token T also contains the file index information and t_s indicating the expiration time of the token. The Parse (input) extracts timestamp ts, token T, signature S, and index Φ from a download request. The function Match (T, t_s, K) checks the token T against public key K. Similarly, Match (S, p) grants access if S matches with p.

3.4 NUMERICAL ANALYSIS

The simulation is conducted in Java which estimates the shortest feasible download time by a pirate or by any normal clients. The simulation is carried out using 100–500 nodes connected in P2P network considering 100 transactional rounds. Practically, the download time should be highly increased for the case of unauthorized clients present in the network. The simulation is initiated by considering distributing agent to have a possession of clean chunks. The proposed simulation test bed has consideration of various challenging scenarios of piracy for understand the efficiency of the framework designed. Fig. 3.8 shows the simulation results considering average path length, network diameter, and algorithm for identity based signature and non-indexed system.

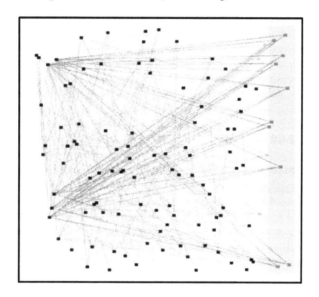

Figure 3.8: Simulation output showing peer

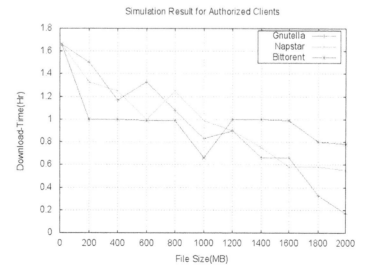

Figure 3.9: Simulation result for authorized clients

Table 3.1: Simulation result for authorized clients

X	10	200	400	600	800	1000	1200	1400	1600	1800	2000
Gnutella	1.66	1.50	1.17	1.33	1.08	0.83	0.90	0.66	0.66	0.33	0.17
Napstar	1.66	1.33	1.25	1.00	1.25	0.99	0.90	0.75	0.58	0.58	0.55
BT	1.66	1.00	1.00	0.99	0.99	0.66	1.00	1.00	0.99	0.80	0.78

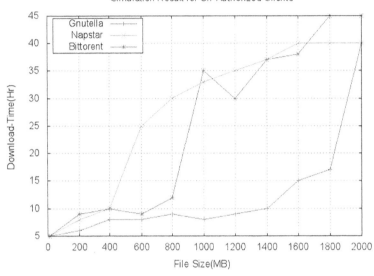

Figure 3.10: Simulation result for un-authorized clients

Table 3.2: Simulation result for un-authorized clients

X	10	200	400	600	800	1000	1200	1400	1600	1800	2000
Gnutella	5	6	8	8	9	8	9	10	15	17	40
Napstar	5	8	10	25	30	33	35	37	40	40	40
BT	5	9	10	9	12	35	30	37	38	45	45

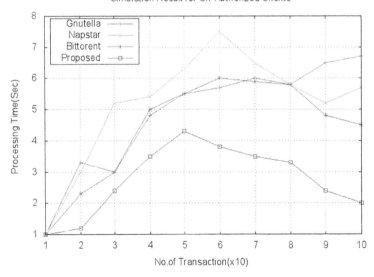

Figure 3.11: Simulation result for un-authorized clients

Table 3.3: Simulation result for un-authorized clients

X	1	2	3	4	5	6	7	8	9	10
Gnutella	1	3.3	3	4.8	5.5	5.7	6	5.8	6.5	6.7
Napstar	1	3	5.2	5.4	6.3	7.5	6.5	5.8	5.2	5.7
BT	1	2.3	3	5	5.5	6	5.9	5.8	4.8	4.5
Proposed	1	1.2	2.4	3.5	4.3	3.8	3.5	3.3	2.4	2

Any frequently used P2P protocol like Bit Torrent or Nap Star could be used for the purpose of simulation. The distribution is evaluated for 2 GB of a multimedia file downloaded from youtube.com. The proposed system is also evaluated with the other different size of the file which have different contents (other than multimedia). Understanding the security implementation of the proposed protocol, it has been seen that when the download request is originated from any client, the proposed framework will first attempt to evaluate the secure confidential identity of the peer nodes and once the authentication is positively accomplished, the cleaner chunk of the digital content requested by the authorized client starts downloading whereas the unauthorized clients will end-up either downloading a poisoned chunks of digital data which will render the unauthorized client to increase the download time to higher extent.

It is clearly observed in Fig. 3.9 that when the experiment is performed with 3 prominent P2P protocols e.g. Bit Torrent, Nap Star, and Gnutella, it can be seen that download time is reduced with every bytes of download of clean chunk of digital contents. While reverse event is witness in case of unauthorized clients as shown in Fig. 3.10, where it can be seen that the download time increase with every bits of download of poisoned chunk of data. Fig. 3.11 highlights the time complexity of the proposed system compared with frequently used P2P protocols like Bit Torrent, Gnutella, and Napster. The outcome highlights that Gnutella protocol suffers from the scalability issues and consumes maximum bandwidth for which processing time is quite higher. Napster suffers from complex client/server protocol with central site for which purpose, extra processing time is required compared to Gnutella. Compared to Gnutella and Nap Star, frequently used Bit Torrent protocol is found to have less processing time.

3.5 CONCLUSION

The chapter basically highlights a novel approach for discriminating authorized and unauthorized peer client in the network. The main intention is to discourage the attempt of any illegitimate client to download the legal and premium content of the digital file on which only the legitimate client have the rights to download. The approach discussed identifies the legal and illegal client and once successful identification is accomplished, the proposed algorithm sends the poisoned chunk of data to the unauthorized client and clean chunk of the digital data only for the genuine and legal peer node. Simulation results claims to highlights the efficiency of proposed algorithm. The proposed system considers hypothetical file size that discretely doesn't consider video and image file as the study focuses more on security technique formulation. The next formulation discussed in consecutive chapter, however, evaluates security standards using video file in P2P network.

CHAPTER 4

FRAMEWORK FOR SECURE ROUTING

4.1 OVERVIEW

This part of the book introduces an analytical design modelling which provides secure routing mechanism in peer-to-peer network. In P2P networks the design aspects of routing paths invites various malicious attacks owing to its vulnerability.

Hence, this book chapter aims to formulate a secure mechanism where the routing mechanism is provided with higher level of confidentiality, privacy, and non-repudiation.

Peer-to-peer network has attracted lots of researchers in last decade with respect to its access to its digital contents via file download, upload, and sharing process. Apart from downloading different types of software's, applications, executables, P2P network is also known for its streaming and multicast, which can cater up the needs of large scale clients, jointly with their security to mix, trustworthiness, and cost effectiveness which are some of the factors why P2P network is preferred mostly in comparison to client-server architecture or other types of content delivery networks. But, unfortunately, it is very difficult and tough to ensure security to Peer-to-Peer application as it is very easy to initiate attack or introduce malware inside the network.

According to the previous researches, P2P multimedia streaming is one of the most difficult area in comparison to other Peer-to-Peer application as they are quite susceptible to quality of service variations. One such issue in delay or jitter which resist the delivery of digital content to the paid customers, which is the most preferred time to initiate any malicious program. Any peer connected with the victim peer will also undergo the damage, there the damage is extremely expensive. Another security issue is related to the OSI layers of P2P network, which renders transport and network layer vulnerable for external attacks. Various types of smart malicious programs can manage to attack or intrude selectively the assurance that the streaming conference should facilitate, which causes some digital contents to be corrupted. It can also make the digital content unavailable to specific digital contents. Therefore, it has been seen that Peer-To-Peer network area majorly consists of illegitimate digital contents as no security algorithms is facilitated in order to ensure the genuinely of the digital contents distribution in these networks. There are various organizations which attempted to deploy the peer-to-peer technology which claims to provide the video streaming services in P2P architecture. However, due to its success, it rapidly loaded underlying physical networks because the peer selection algorithm did not take into consideration the underlying networks (because there were no cooperation between the P2P providers and the network operators).

Unfortunately, due to the existence of such limitations, the service providers as well as original content providers are quite hesitant to organize and utilize P2P liberation. Those two limitations make that content providers as well as network operators are still reluctant to deploy and use a P2P delivery system because of security issues (legality of content, security of the system that can be attacked or infected) and load of the network (since no network-awareness in the peer selection). Such type so applications will target to introduce a secure system in order to represents those two restricting these two limiting points and thus provides secure and legal network aware P2P multimedia systems.

4.2 AN INSIGHT INTOANALYITCAL DESIGN FOUNDATION

This segment of the study discusses the essential goal of the proposed P2P communication systems which formulates a security measures towards protection of digital contents in Peer-to-Peer Network. The architecture of the system is composed of the functional blocks presented in Figure 4.1. Firstly the user should download the P2P software client from an e-tailer (Content provider) who is directly in relation with the end consumer through his own portal. A certificate is delivered to the user by the certification authority after identification. The certification authority validates the P2P software clients that are allowed to access the system.

After choosing contents to be downloaded, a content download requests are directly send to the management server. The management server asks the topology server to provide guidance to figure out which peers are better to select from the network perspective. Afterward, the Management Server replies to P2P client with:

1. A description of the content (and possibly the quality) to be downloaded, allowing reconstructing content once downloaded every chunk,
2. A list of P2P software clients that constitute its new peer-set. The content preparation server cuts contents into chunks.

The list of the chunks related to a given content is built, signed and transmitted to the Management server. This list contains the associated content ID, the chunk IDs and the chunk hashes. Later, the chunks will be transmitted in the network independently; some chunks of the content can have different paths as others of the same video content.

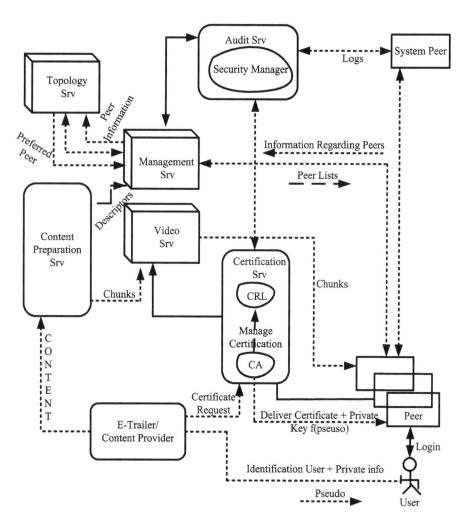

Figure 4.1: Architecture of the P2P Images system

Security is conducted by the audit server. All logs from entities of the system (System peers, Management Severs, all other servers) are sent to the audit server. The latter runs a security manager which analyzes logs and collected alarms to inform the management server about malicious peers, possibly to be excluded from peer lists or revoked. System peer is a conventional peer controlled by the system. It is launched by the Security Manager from the Audit Server. System peer behaves like "standard" peer within the swarm, but it sends information about users in the swarms, in which it is connected, to the Audit Server.

4.3 CORE DESIGN METHODOLOGY OF THE FRAMEWORK

The components of the analytical design are as followings:-

4.3.1 Connectivity Component

In order to take into account the network-awareness in the peer selection algorithm, cooperation between network operators and service provider is defined. This cooperation leads to two distinct entities: one managed by network operators, called the Topology Server (TS) and one managed by service providers, called the Management Server (MS) (see Fig. 4.1). The Topology Server (TS) role is to maintain an accurate view of its network topology, with list of IP networks (or IP addresses) associated to different network groups (e.g., ADSL Points of presence or groups of cities) and weighted links for connecting them.

Those weighted links are based on value of metrics such as bandwidth, delay, availability of links, cost of links, etc. The network topology information also encompasses information about peering relationships (i.e., if the operator has special agreements with some others operators). Based on this network topology, the TS will return back to the MS (step 3) a list of preferred peers to select, when requesting by the MS (step 2).

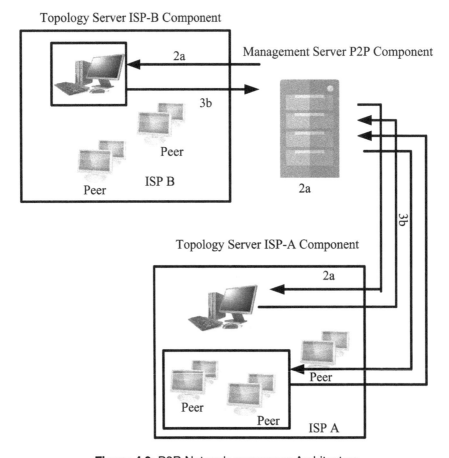

Figure 4.2: P2P Network-awareness Architecture

The Management Server (MS) is the P2P central entity which will provide the list of peers (step 4) when a peer joins the P2P network (step 1). Instead of sending peers selected randomly (from the list of peers sharing the contents) or based on application-level consideration, the MS will choose the peers that are preferred by the network operators, via a request/response protocol on a well-defined interface to the TS (step 2 and 3 in figure 4.2).

The interface between the MS and TS has two simple methods:

> *Connect (infohash, ip)*: which allows the MS to inform the TS that a new peer (with this "ip" address) is joining the swarm identified by "infohash" and get back a list of preferred peers (to network operators point of view) who are in the same swarm.
> *Deconnect (infohash, ip)*: which allows the MS to inform the TS that a peer (with this "ip" address) is leaving the swarm identified by "infohash."

In this interface, information such as the content (identified by info hash value) or the end-user (identified by its IP address) is passed to the TS. Some people may object about it since it could be against user privacy but since the goal of the prototype is the delivery of a secure and legal content, having this information could help to control the legality of the content as well as the client.

4.3.2 Core Framework Component

The system is for delivering the requested multimedia content. Peer client software should then be adapted for proposed multimedia on demand requirements; i.e., chunks download should be ordered to get chunks sequentially (or close to it) and not get chunks randomly. Instead of starting from crash, it adapts the Bit Torrent Open Source code, developed in the Python Language, which is performing well, support large number of clients and is reliable. The modifications we did consist of adaptations of the ranking of chunks index in Bit Torrent buckets and the organization of the bucket of buckets, whose main interest is to manage the priority of chunks. The chunks are then organized in order to have sequential and not random chunk download. We also added a sliding window for the chunks download (this window can depend on the play-out time). All chunks that are within this window are preferably (and sometimes urgently) required are organized accordingly in the buckets. When all chunks are downloaded, the windows moves and then the following chunks are requested. In the implementation, we define the window as the size of 50 chunks. In order to watch the video content, the peer software includes a wrapper to VLC player. Adaptation has been made in order to have player automatically started as soon as enough data has been downloaded by the peer. One main concern for the peer implementation was to reduce as much as possible this delay between the start of the download and the play-out of the video. Finally, since the system is for secure and legal video content delivery, some added-value functions for security have been added: the watermarking function and the authentication module.

4.3.3 Core Multimedia Watermarking Component

Legal video distribution usually comes with content protection technologies, especially with Digital Rights Management (DRM). This kind of protection is very restrictive for the customer, since it only works with compatible systems, players and devices. Thus, we decided to use a system-agnostic content protection system based on digital watermarking. Digital watermarking consists in embedding invisible information within content samples, i.e., pixels for image and video. This information must be robust: even if marked content is processed (e.g., video compression), we must be able to reliably read embedded data. Digital watermarking can deal with video, sound and pictures. Nevertheless, the algorithm we describe here can only handle images and video. Figure 4.3 depicts the defined watermarking algorithm. Given an image to be watermarked, its 8 × 8 Discrete Cosine

Transform (DCT) is computed [1]. This transformed domain was chosen because it is also used for MPEG video compression algorithms and allows the design of less visible marks. Selected DCT coefficients are projected on pseudo-random carriers thanks to a spread transform. Carriers are computed from a secret key. This leads to the host vector denoted x.

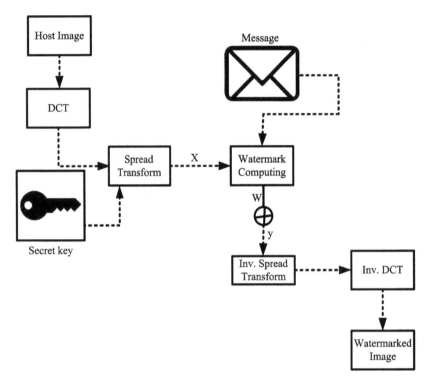

Figure 4.3: Watermarking Algorithm

The watermark vector w is obtained from x and the message m to be embedded using a Turbo Trellis Coded Quantization (TTCQ) algorithm [2][3]: this coding technique provided state-of-the-art watermarking robustness. Finally, w is added to x, then inverse spread transform and inverse DCT are computed, leading to the watermarked image. The watermark reading function uses same steps: image DCT then spread transform. TTCQ algorithm is then used to decode the message from y = x + w. In the system, each video frame is watermarked with 20-bits long message. The same message is used for all frames. Robustness benchmark done with SD movies shows that the message can be recovered even if watermarked movies are compressed with MPEG-4 at 200 Kb/s rate (very poor video quality).

Watermarking function is integrated within peers' video player (VLC player). After video decoding, images are watermarked prior to display. The embedded message corresponds to the peer's certificate. Thus, if a movie is illegally distributed, we can find out the client who leaked it. Each distributed movie copy is then unique thanks to watermarking. In order to detect illegal copies, we use system peers, deployed in the network. While DRM protections are often seen as a major drawback of legal distribution platforms (because the technologies are not compatible with each other and sometimes prohibit legitimate uses of content), the watermarking technology we use is a transparent form of protection for video. The user can convert copy and read watermarked movies on any player or system. But he knows that if he illegally distributes the content he bought, he may be accused. Of course, customers must be notified in advance of the operation of protection under the conditions of use of the platform.

4.3.4 Core Security Component

The aim of the security in this study is (1) to authenticate users, in order to allow only authorized people to join the system, (2) to verify the identity of passing content to allow only authorized content to be exchange,

(3) to analyze the flows exchanged between the various entities in the system (including peers) to detect malicious behaviors that may attack the system or alter its efficiency.

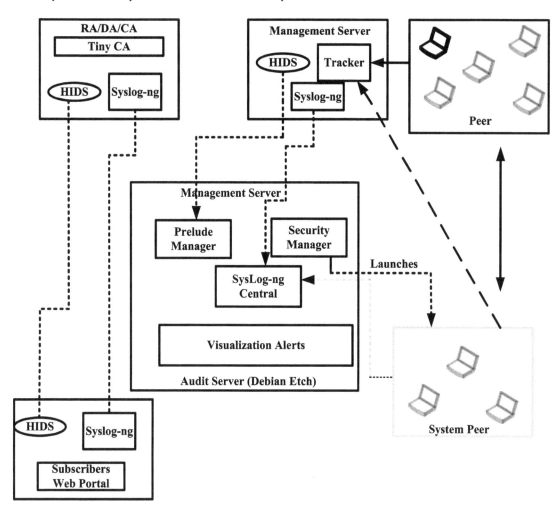

Figure 4.4: Security Detection System

In order to identify and authenticate entities in the system, two mechanisms have been identified: Secure Sockets Layer (SSL) communication and the use of certificates. Each software client needs to acquire a certificate to be able to access the system. A unique ID (called Client SoftwareID) is attributed to each software client. The ID is directly taken from the Registration Certification Authority (RCA). All certificates are generated off-line by the Certificate Authority (CA) and transmitted to the RCA. The CA keeps track of all Client SoftwareID to be sure they remain unique. The ClientSoftwareID can be revoked by the CA if the owner of that certificate behaves maliciously (e.g., id detected by system peers, see below). In order to detect malicious behaviors, information about peers are collected by so-called System Peers and gathered and analyzed by the Audit Server. A System peer is a peer controlled by the system. It is launched by the Security Manager from the Audit Server. In the swarm the system peer behaves like any standard peer but when communicating with others peers, it collects information about them and sends it to the Audit Server.

When a Security manager activates a System Peers it gives them a swarm target. Several attacks can be detected directly by the System. Peer or through the correlation of logs sends by several System Peers, such as free rider attacks, network flooding attacks, network filtering, incorrect use of the protocol. Statistical analysis is recovered by the Audit server that can decide, depending on the event, to take some actions (alerting peer, revoking it, etc.). Several techniques to restrict access to malicious peers are used according to the gravity of the behavior. The various entities that send logs to the Audit server are shown in Figure 4.6. The Host Intrusion Detection System (HIDS) alarms sent by authentication components (Registration Authority, Delivery Authority and Certification Authority) (RA, DA, CA) to the Audit Server are already encrypted (use of prelude manager tools). All information sent to the Audit Server are on an encrypted Syslog channel.

4.4 PERFORMANCE ANALYSIS AND OUTCOME

The main target of the evaluation was to identify the quality of the content that can be delivered to end-users enjoying the services in a real-life configuration. This mainly means end-users connected behind an Internet Box (e.g., Livebox) at a given throughput (e.g., 1 or 10 Mbit/s) using a real ISP connection. Several clients in different locations (8 in Lannion with 2 dedicated for the MS and the TS, 2 in Rennes, 6 in Nantes, with 3 dedicated for the System peers) were used in order to have a distributed network.

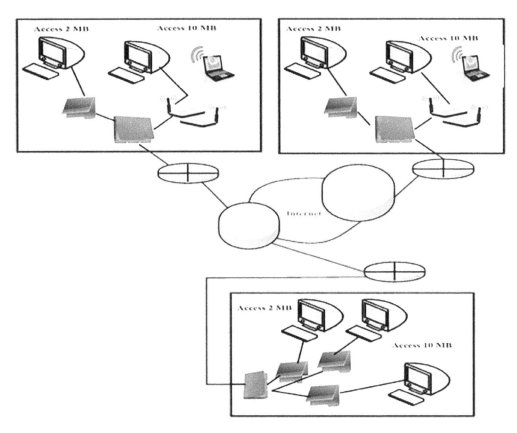

Figure 4.5: Performance Evaluation test bed

The quality of the video has been evaluated in an objective way; the end-users themselves will note the quality of the video, according to the MOS scale. Fig. 4.5 depicts this environment in the end-user side. In the current implementation, the MS and the TS are written in the Python language. The network topology is a text file, which is updated according to network conditions changes. The interfaces between the MS and TS are sockets and data are formatted using JSON (JavaScript Object Notation) for transmission. We made different tests for evaluating the quality of video as well as the efficiency of the system regarding security issues.

For the video quality, we made tests with peers wanting the content (video is watched during downloading) in Lannion and Rennes using 1M and 10M links and with one peer offering the content (seeder) located in Lannion. Following table shows the results.

Table 4.1: Download time & Play out

Client	Complete Download in	Video Player starts after
Lannion 10M	3'20"	15"
Lannion 1M	14'	1'15" (player blocked, buffer empty waiting data)
Rennes 10M	3'46"	22"

This test proved that the download of a video in a P2P fashion is feasible for users having a high bandwidth within a good time and that the end-users does not have to wait for a long time before the start of the video (time needed to fill in the buffer). After the start of the video, the video is smoothly played-out without any interruption or freeze. But users being 1M links cannot watch the video smoothly since the link is too slow (buffer empty, waiting for data). For video quality, we made tests to evaluate the behavior of the client on interrupted session. Whereas the interruption occurred because of end-users stop or because of a network failure, the download restarted where it was (not starting from the beginning).

For the tests highlighting the network-awareness of the solution, we used peers located in the three sites: Lannion, Rennes and Nantes, and having links between sites with different priority based on the cost of using the physical link: (1) higher priority level for link Rennes-Nantes, (2) medium priority for link Lannion-Rennes, (3) lower priority level for link Lannion-Nantes. It means that link Lannion-Nantes should be avoided as often as possible.

We have tested different scenario such as: one seeder was started in Nantes, one client (lecher) was started in Lannion; since no local seeder is available then the seeder in Nantes was selected,

One seeder as started in Lannion: the peer in Lannion must connect to seeder in Lannion and disconnect from seeder in Nantes as soon as possible, one peer was started in Rennes: it must be connected to seeder Nantes (higher priority). or others with the requirement to have at least several seeders for a good delivery of video, such as: we started one seeder in Nantes and one in Lannion, we started one client peer in Lannion: downloading from seeders in Nantes and Lannion, start a new Seeder in Lannion: Peer in Lannion must to connect to new seeder in Lannion, must disconnect from seeder in Nantes. In all cases, the tests were successful and the disconnection/reconnection from/to seeders was done transparently to end-users, and not detectable since the video quality was good, without freeze nor blocking artifacts. Those tests proved that the topology-awareness when selecting peers help in reducing network bandwidth and has also no impact in the end-user QoE. The change of one seeder to another one does not lead to freeze in the video. The apparition of one seeder in the region is automatically detected and the lecher peer connects to this new local seeder and disconnect from remote seeder. Security tests were more functional tests, aiming at checking the efficiency of the implemented solutions to detect and mitigate illegal behavior of peers. An interface was developed to conduct tests on the security platform. A Bash file is generated through this interface and run on the security platform. Logs of machines concerned by the test are displayed trough this interface. All tests were conducted with 8 machines (1 MS, 3 Peers, 3 Systems Peers). Audit Server and Security Manager were on the same machine. All the functional tests were successful. The tests we have done are:

➤ Flooding of secure connections detection: The System Peer relates this attack to Audit Server when it receives lots of secure connections in a small amount of time.

➤ Network flooding detection: The audit server (Security Manager) can detect a network flooding attack by correlating logs coming from System Peers. The System Peer can report a Free-Rider peer by analyzing its behavior. The audit Server takes a decision concerning this peer if the same behavior is reported by the other System Peers.

> ➢ Detection of an incorrect use of P2PIm@ges protocol: System Peer analyse all messages exchanged with peers. If the protocol used by the peer is incorrect, the system peer sends logs to the Audit Server with information (IP, CN, etc.) of the concerned peer. After that, the revocation of the certificate of peer is performed by the Audit Server.

> ➢ Detection of compromised certificate/ private keys: The misbehavior is detected when an attacker tries periodically to connect to the MS with a bad or expired certificate (Certification authority not recognized). This lead to (1) connection refused by Tracker, (2) message displayed with IP of Attacker and (3) after several tries, attacker IP is blocked.

SSL flooding attacks type "Denial of Server" (DoS) on protected servers are detected when attacker tries periodically to the MS without certificate. The connection is refused ans the peer IP is blocked after several tries. For watermarking tests, we made tests aiming at evaluating the amount of time needed to detect a watermark from the beginning of the downloading process. System peers provide a watermark detection daemon, which checks video chunks during their download. If a watermark is detected, an alert is sent to security logger with the extracted ID and movie file name.

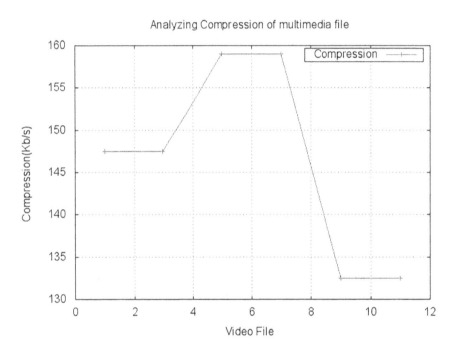

Figure 4.6: Analyzing Compression of multimedia file

Table 4.2: Analyzing Compression of multimedia file

Video File	1	3	5	7	9	11
Compression	147.5	147.5	159	159	132.5	132.5

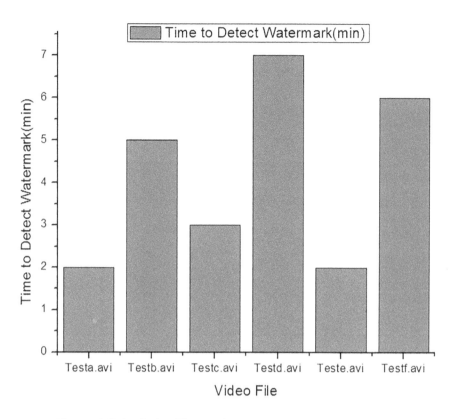

Figure 4.7: Analyzing Time to detect watermarking in minutes

Figure 4.6 shows that need of compression is found maximized for first four video samples while it decreases with remaining video files. Figure 4.7 shows that time to detect watermark highly varies from 2minutes to 7 minutes. For this test, we limited the upload/download rate to 20 Kb/s for all peers. The following results were obtained, depending of the file size (3 files) and the number of system peers that were used (1 or 3 system peers). This test proved that the system can detect illegal content in the P2P network quite quickly. It is longer when several peers are used because correlation is done between information provided by system peers. A compromise is made between detection accuracy and detection time; in those results, we focused on very low false detection rates. The preliminary evaluation was done to understand the extent of payoff gained by different watermarking methods is to the maximum value. The best benefit gain in this study is evaluated as follows. At each temporal iteration, it is assumed that a virtual seed server that is designed by gathering the competence of all peers as well as the authentic seed server, ignoring all data accessibility constraints at peers. Therefore, the optimal payoff that can be benefited using the virtual seed server is maximum than or equal to the optimal payoff that can be actually benefited from the network.

Since exploring the optimal payoff of the virtual seed server is an NP-complete problem [47], the study assumes the optimal answer of the LP-relaxation of the problem, which is at least as large as the actual optimal utility. Thus, the best payoff that we consider can be an upper bound on the highest payoff that can be benefited in the network.

The theoretical approximation ratio for this evaluation is considered as highest, while we see it has reached slightly lower values in practice. This is due to dynamics of the network that were not involved in the approximation analyses, i.e., the experimental ratio would have been always higher that 96% if all peers stayed in the network as expected, they let the tracker (and the tracker was able to) decide and update their partnerships at every 10-second step, and all peers did obey the assumptions about sharing their upload bandwidths among layers, which we intentionally made them disobey by deviating by up to 50% from their supposed values. The study also depicts that the two approximation algorithms operate almost equally efficiently for a seed server capacity of 10.5 Mbps; since the network consists of hundreds of peers we do not consider seeding capacities below 10.5 Mbps as such seed servers will not be practical. For larger capacities, the dynamic algorithm takes a significant time to operate with reasonable approximation factor. Thus, we do not consider this method in the following evaluations as they deal with large seeding capacities.

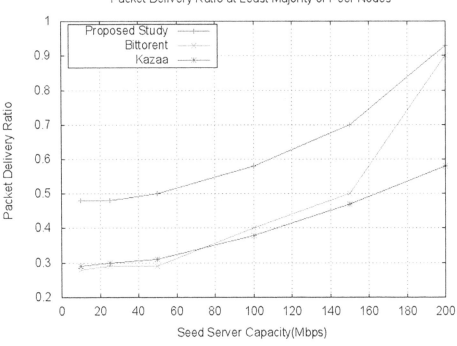

Figure 4.8: Packet Delivery Ratio at least majority of peer nodes

Table 4.3: Packet Delivery Ratio at least majority of peer nodes

X	10	25	50	100	150	200
Proposed	0.48	0.48	0.50	0.58	0.7	0.93
Bittorent	0.28	0.29	0.29	0.40	0.50	0.90
Kazaa	0.29	0.30	0.31	0.38	0.47	0.58

We now assess the maximization in the overall peer satisfaction, which is the fraction that a peer receives out of its demanded video quality. Figure 4.8 shows the packet delivery ratio by at least 91.2% of peer nodes. The proposed study is evaluated with Bit Torrent protocol, Kazaa protocol, and proposed study.

The proposed system exponentially increases the packet delivery ratio especially for limited seeding capacities, which is often the case in practice. Figure 4.7 also exhibits that for a very large seeding capacity such as 210 Mbps, which is nearly enough for fully catering up the services of all peers even with the Bit Torrent protocol, the Bit Torrent-like method still could not increase the packet delivery ratio as expected. That is because this technique followed a random peer matching, which caused unproductive exploitation of peer nodes and their respective resources. In the consecutive phase, the proposed study evaluates the multimedia quality delivered to peers.

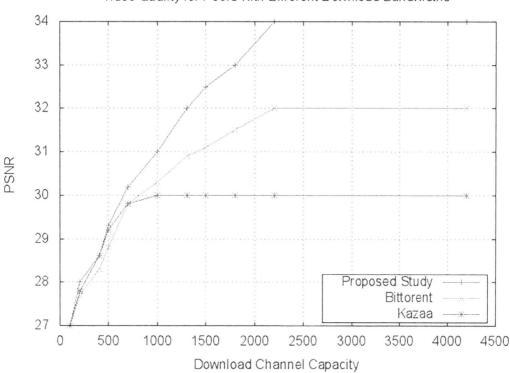

Figure 4.9: Video Quality for peers with different download bandwidths

Table 4.4: Video Quality for peers with different download bandwidths

X	100	200	400	500	700	1000	1300	1500	1800	2200	4200
Proposed	27	28	28.6	29.3	30.2	31	32	32.5	33	34	34
Bittorent	27	27.7	28.3	28.8	29.8	30.3	30.9	31.1	31.5	32	32
Kazaa	27	27.8	28.6	29.2	29.8	30	30	30	30	30	30

Figure 4.9 depicts the average PSNR that represents the quality of different downloaded multimedia files. The seed server capacity is 27 Mbps. Without the proposed algorithm, some superior quality levels could not be accomplished at all (beyond 30 dB). The other superiority levels would require peer nodes to have a considerably larger channel capacity, e.g., beyond 3 Mbps for a quality of 33 dB whereas it is accomplished by 1.3 Mbps by using the proposed system. A quality maximization of more than 3 dB is accomplished for most of the peer elements; the quality range of the considered scalable video is 12 dB in total.

The proposed result analysis can be discussed as due to the considered system, a request is responded with a delay of up to the phase between allocation algorithm iterations. This duration is typically a few seconds, but it is 10 seconds in the experiments; it needs to be this large so that the simulator, which is both in charge of allocation tasks as well as tasks of hundreds of peers, can simulate the network in reasonable time. Nevertheless, even the heavily-loaded Java simulation was able to perform such computations faster than real-time. The proposed system relies on extracting and utilizing the upload channel capacity of peers.

This could be a weakness if peers are not cooperative. It is feasible that one might debate that this result is because peer nodes with higher upload channel capacity also have higher download capacity, and naturally receive more multimedia layers. We see, however, that for methods BitTorrent and Kazaa-like this superiority difference is very marginal and the received superiority is almost independent of the upload channel capacity.

Thus, the higher superiority accomplished by the proposed secure system is mainly due to cooperation and secure routing between two peer nodes. With the proposed study compared to BitTorrent and Kazaa-like algorithms, cooperating peers receive up to 8 dB higher quality, which is even more than half of the entire superiority range of the video. This clearly shows the provided protocol not only ensures security but also maintains quality of the multimedia transmission over P2P network.

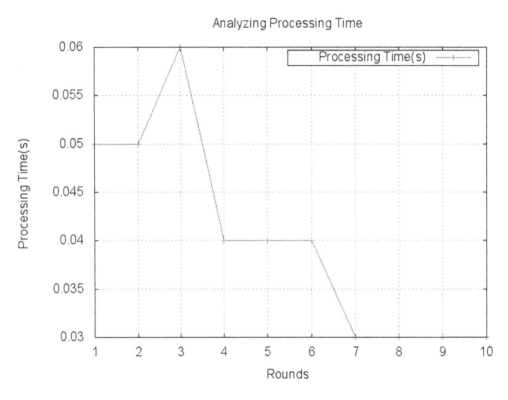

Figure 4.10: Analyzing Processing time

Table 4.5: Analyzing Processing time

X	1	2	3	4	5	6	7	8	9	10
Proposed	0.1	0.2	0.3	0.3	0.4	0.5	0.6	0.8	0.9	0.9

Figure 4.10 shows the result accomplished after performing the simulation study to see that the processing time of the proposed system is highly optimized while maintaining a better uniformity in the processing time. The variable rounds specify the number of iterations that were made to understand the variation of processing time of the proposed system considering different files. Hence, increased in rounds also signifies increase in complexities involved in processing the proposed system. The basic reason behind this is the modified usage of hash function using if SHA1 or MD5 that is used for performing sender ambiguity for which literally no keys are stored in any database. The keys are generated, released, used, and eroded to make the processing time quite faster.

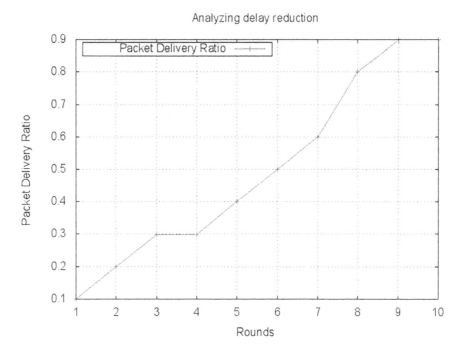

Figure 4.11: Analyzing delay reduction

Table 4.6: Analyzing delay reduction

X	1	2	3	4	5	6	7	8	9	10
Proposed	0.1	0.2	0.3	0.3	0.4	0.5	0.6	0.8	0.9	0.9

Figure 4.11 highlights the results accomplished from the simulation study that analyzes delay reduction. Another interesting fact to note from this study is that although the non-complicated model of P2P is deployed in the proposed system, the proposed algorithm are actually built on the top of frequently used P2P applications like gtalk, BitTorrent, Limewire, Gnutella, etc. the efficient secure scheme ensures exponential safety using watermarking by maintaining the visual quality of multimedia files.

4.5 CONCLUSION

In this chapter of the book, a secure and legal network-aware P2P system has been presented. The main goals of this study was: (1) to reduce the network load in the network via a better organization of the P2P network (better peer selection algorithm) while ensuring a good Quality of Experience to end-users, (2) to offer a secure and legal content distribution system that could convince content providers to distribute their contents using a P2P system since solutions to protect them about security issues are provided in the system. In this study, we have assumed streaming of scalable multimedia files over standard P2P networks. In these networks, due to the significant asymmetry between peer nodes download and upload channel capacity, a quantity of seed servers need to be used in the network for delivering high-class video streams to peer nodes. The study has focused on the issues of assigning these seeding resources to the requests of peers for different sub-streams, in order to exploit a system-wide payoff function. Such issues can be represented as NP-complete. The simulation results confirm that the payoff accomplished by the proposed study is always beyond 91% of the best payoff that can be benefited from the proposed. The results exhibits also that the proposed seed server provisioning protocols result in peers receiving more multimedia layers, and thus an improved multimedia quality over 3 dB. The evaluation that has been performed both in lab and in a real-life configuration (end-users behind DSL boxes and interconnected via

Internet) proved the quality of the prototype and the efficiency of the proposed system. It has also proved that technologies exist and can be deployed for delivering video content in a secure way. The next step is to convince content providers as well as network operators to widely deploy such systems.

REFERENCES

[1]   Tien Tuan AnhDinh and Mark Ryan, "Checking Security Property of P2P Systems Using CSP"

[2]   Michele Amoretti, "A Survey of Peer-to-Peer Overlay Schemes: Effectiveness, Efficiency and Security," Recent Patents on Computer Science 2009

[3]   Markus Fiedler, CharlottEliasson, Tomasz Ciszkowski, WojciechMazurczyk and ZbigniewKotulski, "Parameterisation of a reputation system for VoIP in P2P networks for improved communication quality and security, BTH/EuroFGI, 2008

CHAPTER 5

An Efficient Computational Model for Resisting Malicious Payload Insertion

5.1 OVERVIEW

This chapter introduces a framework that is efficient for mitigating the fatal attack generated by any illegitimate peers in P2P network. The model is constructed using cryptographic hash tags that enable the security principles such as privacy, confidentiality of the multimedia packets being transmitted over P2P network.

Peer-to-peer systems have gained more and more momentum over the last years as a means to access multimedia contents, albeit initially in form of file downloads. The evolution to streaming and multicast (e.g., TV) was just a consequence. The P2P (Peer-to-Peer) technology is now well-known by the public, mainly because of the great success of some applications, such as file sharing applications (Kazaa, eDonkey, BitTorrent, etc.) but also more recently such as video streaming applications (PPLive, PPStream, UUSee, SopCast, etc. [1][2]). However, the P2P networks still suffer from bad reputation because of the large number of illegal contents that are distributed by those applications. For instance, for video streaming, major companies fear to have their contents "pirated" and redistributed without respecting the digital rights. Several research works proposed solutions for a P2P video delivery but do not really take into consideration the legal aspects of it [1][3][4]. Their power to accommodate large amounts of users, together with their resilience to churn, reliability, and low cost are some of the reasons why they are preferred over dedicated servers or content distribution solutions. In spite of these advantages, some P2P features make these systems more difficult to defend against some classes of attacks. Security-wise, P2P streaming systems are more challenging than other P2P applications because they are more vulnerable to QoS fluctuations. Live streaming protocols and TV in particular are most sensitive to delay and delay jitter. If some other peers are connected to that machine, they will be damaged as well. Apart from their time-sensitive nature and bandwidth dependency, P2P streaming is susceptible to manipulation and threats at the transport and network layers.

Clever attacks can compromise selectively the guarantees that a streaming session should provide, rendering some channels unusable, or making the broadcast unavailable in particular locations. Both events can be classified as targeted censorship violating the freedom of speech and expression. Analyzing the threat models in all these cases gives relevant indicators over possible risks and vulnerabilities in the transmission. One of the prime issues in terms of security in P2P network is the origin of the digital content file. If many nodes behave selfishly by consuming too much bandwidth, then well-behaving nodes might not be able to access media streams that would otherwise be available if all nodes were well-behaved. If one or more nodes exhaust all of the available upload bandwidth in the P2P media streaming system due to malice, then a denial-of-service (DoS) attack has occurred on the system because other well-behaving nodes will be prevented from downloading media streams.

We propose a P2P system that ensures the security of contents, by controlling that only authorized contents are exchanged between peers and by being able to identify the people that redistribute illegal contents if it happens. This is mostly addressed by the use of watermarking functions in the video contents processing and by the deployment of specific peers that can monitor and detect misbehavior of the peers.

5.2 DESIGN CONSIDERATION FOR RESISTING MALICIOUS PAYLOAD INSERTION

The prime objective of the designed system is to construct a secure model in peer-to-peer system that can provide secure encryption for the transmitted video content. The attack scenario of malicious payload insertion by illegal peer is considered for the study.

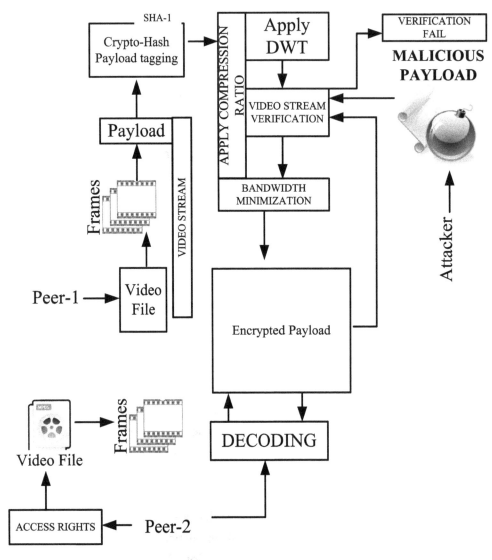

Figure 5.1: Design of System against Malicious Payload Insertion

The system goal is to serve multi-media content from a source to a client. The model assumes that the content comes into existence at the source, i.e. it is not required to consider storing and securing the media at the origin. Furthermore, it is assumed that there is just one original source, but that there are many clients that want to receive the data. The work carried in this chapter is specifically geared towards being able to scale effortlessly to support millions of clients without prior notice, i.e. be able to handle a "mob-like" behavior of the clients. Some lag time between creation of source data and its consumption by clients is acceptable, but excessive wait will defeat the attractiveness of the approach. The presented schema is as shown in Fig. 5.1.

Conventional P2P approaches that are frequent in use are considered. The source data is made available at a preset quality using a variable-rate video encoder. The source data stream is divided into fixed length sequential frames: each frame is identified by it frame number and encrypted. Clients request frames in sequence, decrypt the frame and reassemble the video stream which is then displayed using a suitable video decoder and display utility. The video stream is encoded in such a fashion that missing frames don't prevent a resulting video to be shown, but rather a video of lesser bit-rate encoding, i.e. quality, will result. Multi-media sources are advertised and made available via a central tracking service: at first, this tracker only knows the network tracker location of the server. Clients that want to access the source do so via the tracker: they contact the tracker that will respond with the location of the source. The tracker will also remember (or track) the clients as potential new sources of the data. Subsequent client requests to the tracker are answered with all known locations of sources: the original and the known client. Clients that receive locations of sources from the tracker issue frame requests immediately to all sources. Clients will also answer requests for frames that they have received already, which will enable a cascading effect, which establishes a P2P network where each client is a peer. For better encoding, each frame is processed using discrete wavelet transform.

The image payload is reconstructed exclusively from the packets that are received, decoded, and verified at the recipient peer end. In order to maximize the expected cumulative distortion reduction that will mean indirectly to increase the quality, one can make use of cypto-hash link parents and control the wireless network resources in P2P application e.g. modulation and retransmission.

$$\{a_{1,i}, r_{l,i}, m_{\max}\} = \arg\max\{[\Delta D]\} \tag{5.1}$$

Where $l \in \{0, 1...L-1\}$ and $i \in \{0, 1...N_{l-1}\}$. The above equation (1) should comply with the total bandwidth constraint as given by,

$$B_{tot} = \sum_{l=0}^{L-} \sum_{i=0}^{N_{l-1}} B_{l,i} \tag{5.2}$$

$$B_{tot} \leq B_{\max}$$

With a specified payload distortion reduction requirement ($\Delta D_{l,i}$) a cumulative payload delivery probability $\theta_{l,i}$ and a verification probability $v(a_{l,i})$ with respect to crypto-hash parent selection $a_{l,i}$, once can express the expected authenticated distortion reduction as:

$$\varepsilon[\Delta D] = \sum_{l=0}^{L-1} \sum_{i=0}^{N_{l-1}} \Delta D_{l,i} \theta_{l,i} v(a_{l,i}) \tag{5.3}$$

i.e. $[\Delta D]$ = [payload distortion reduction requirement]x[cumulative packet delivery probability]x[verification probability]. The work done in [5] signifying image decoding quality gain is considered for framing up equation (5.1), (5.2), and (5.3) for evaluation of image payload distortion reduction. Hence, the issue in image transmission in error prone channel of P2P network is classified as 3 sub-determinants (see figure 5.1):

> ➢ Inborn decoding dependence that is used to evaluate the total payload delivery probability.
> ➢ Additional authentication dependency for determining verification probability $v(a_{1,i})$.
> ➢ Bandwidth consumption $(B_{1,i})$ at link layer for each packet delivery.

It is very important to understand that it is not feasible to design an overall optimal authentication hash graphs for all the massive size of image payloads in P2P network. The prime reason behind this is that image payloads are highly interdependent due to decoding dependency that also gives great potential to simplify the network authentication design. Therefore, the proposed system uses JPEG2000 encoding and decoding schema [6] as here the decoding of each high definition (HD) layer packets depends on successful decoding of those packets in the same code block or sectors from previous quality layer. Hence, it is felt that it is highly reasonable to match the crypto-hash link dependency assignment during the authentication process to the image decoding dependency. Since, the crypto-hash tag of the HD layers is attached to previous layers packet, the authentication rate-distortion performance can be highly optimized. Therefore, it can be said that unification between image payload authentication in P2P network and its decoding is highly challenging task.

Hence, as a part of feasible solution, stream authentication process is simplified to crypto-hash link assignment on layer-0 packets. Furthermore, only one outgoing crypto-hash link needs to be applied to each packet if the whole image is signed only once. For example, let Ω_i denote the set consisting of the entire verification associates of the ith packet in Layer 0 and the said packet itself. If the crypto-hash tag of Packet 4(i=4) is attached to Packet 2 (i=2) and the tag of Packet 2 is attached to Packet 0 (i=0, i.e., the root signature packet), then the framework can have the ancestor set. This will be one important consideration for mitigating malicious payload insertion. The verified payload quality can be represented as

$$\varepsilon[\Delta D] = \Delta D_{0,0} x(1 - \varsigma_{0,0}) + \sum_{i=1}^{N_0-1} \Delta D_{0,i} \prod_{j \in \Omega_i}(1 - \varsigma_{0,j}) + \sum_{l=1}^{L-1} \sum_{i=0}^{N_l} \Delta D_{l,i} \prod_{k=0}^{l}(1 - \varsigma_{k,i}) x \prod_{j \in \Omega_i}(1 - \varsigma_{0,j}) \quad (5.4)$$

The LHS of eq (5.4) represents total expectation of distortion reduction/quality of the decode frames after packet-by-packet authentication, it is basically represented as:

(packet distortion reduction requirement) x (cumulative packet delivery probability) x (verification probability). It can definitely have summations and multiplication as well as probably more mathematical operation depending on the application design. We are also applying quantization in the application

Hence equation (5.4) is derived from equation (5.3) in higher order. The crypto-hash link assignment for stream authentication generates extra data load in terms of the source encoding overhead (due to the hash tag size Shash and signature size Ssig), resulting in higher communication bandwidth consumption, while the extra data dependency incurs less error resilience during transmissions. Let $|\pi_{l,i}|$ denote the incoming hash link redundancy of the ith packet in Layer l. For example, if Packet 2 in Layer 0 has two authentication descendants (i.e., Packet 3 in Layer 0 and Packet 4 in Layer 0), then the redundancy degree of Packet 2 is $|\pi_{0,2}|=|1+1|=2$. Based on the above analysis, the total bandwidth consumption can be expressed as,

$$B_{tot} = B_{o,o}\left(S_{sig} + |\Pi_{o,o}| S_{hash} + S_{0,o}\right) + \sum_{i=1}^{N_0-1} B_{0,i}\left(|\pi_{o,i}| S_{hash} + S_{0,1}\right) + \sum_{l=1}^{L=2} \sum_{i=0}^{N_l-1} B_{l,i}(S_{hash} + S_{l,i}) + \sum_{i=0}^{N_L-1} B_{L-1},i(S_{L-1,i}) \quad (5.5)$$

A large number of payload packets are present in a compressed video stream, and therefore it is impractical to design an overall optimal verification hash graph for all packets in a low-cost P2P network. Furthermore, the payload packets are interdependent due to the decoding dependency, which provides a great potential to simplify the video stream verification protocol. The presented model contains the decoding of each high-quality-layer payload depends on the successful decoding of those payloads in the same code block or precinct from the previous quality layers. Thus, it is reasonable to match the crypto-hash link dependency assignment during the authentication process to the image decoding dependency. Since the crypto-hash tag of the high-quality-layer's payload is attached to the previous layer's payload, the verification rate-distortion performance can be optimized and there is no extra confirmation dependency overhead incurred.

The framework quantifies the relationship between three factors, i.e., the P2P network resource allocation, the frames distortion during transmission, and the corresponding communication bandwidth consumption. Here, the P2P network resource provision scheme includes the PHY layer transmission power Pt, modulation constellation size b, and MAC retry-limit mmax. The payload distortion is affected dominantly by the average packet loss ratio ξ. Let the average bandwidth consumed by the corresponding video transmission be B. Such a relationship can be derived as follows. The SNR fluctuates in P2P channels due to multi-path propagation, channel attenuation/fading, and interference. There is a performance tradeoff between BER, transmission rate, and the transmission power. By applying multirate-multi-power [7], [8] transmission control, the BER is quantitatively expressed as follows [9]–[10]:

$$e = \frac{2}{b}\left(1 - \frac{1}{2^{b/2}}\right)erfc\left(\sqrt{\frac{3}{2(2^b - 1)}\frac{P_t.A}{R_s N_0}}\right) \tag{5.6}$$

The proposed work has considered QPSK and QAM modulation schemes with an even constellation size (b=2,4,6,8) in a slow fading channel environment as it is one of the most ideal situation for initiating malicious payloads. The proposed system uses QPSK and QAM modulation scheme as it can be used to reduce BER to higher extent. It also enables the system to transmit in the same frequency band twice more information. The loss ratio for a packet with length, given incoming verification redundancy π and transmission overhead Ho and Ha, is expressed as,

$$\xi = 1 - (1 - e)^{S + |\pi| S_{hash} + H_0 + H_a} \tag{5.7}$$

With the increase of incoming authentication redundancy, both packet loss ratio overhead and bandwidth consumption overhead will also be incremented due to the attached crypto-hash tags. The bandwidth consumption of delivering a payload of length can be estimated by

$$B_w = P_t\left(\frac{S + |\pi| S_{hash} + H_0}{R} + T_0\right) + P_r\left(\frac{H_a}{R} + T_0\right) + P_t\left(\frac{H_a}{R} + T_0\right) + P_r\left(\frac{S + |\pi| S_{hash} + H_0}{R} + T_0\right) + 2P_s\left(T\frac{S + |\pi| S_{hash} + H_0 + H_a}{R} - 2T_0\right) \tag{5.8}$$

With the link layer retransmission factor, the average payload loss ratio expectation can be summarized using the following expression,

$$\xi = \xi^{m_{max}} \tag{5.9}$$

Therefore, the bandwidth consumption expectation, [11] can be written as

$$B_w^f = B_w \cdot \frac{1 - \xi^{m_{max}}}{1 - \xi} \tag{5.10}$$

Thus, the packet delivery with distortion-bandwidth performance can be modeled quantitatively as functions ξ and B. These functions should be fine-tuned using transmission control parameters Pt, b, and mmax. The prime objective of the work is to create a framework that can resist malicious payload insertion. Hence, the error prone channel of P2P network (especially wireless) is considered for the purpose of experiment. The experiment is performed considering bandwidth constraint network with payload error rate for assessing the success rate of resisting payload insertion. Due to the usage of crypto-hash link, the transmission performed in the P2P network is ensured private, non-repudiable, and anonymous. The illegal/malicious payload can be easily be authenticated using the parameters considered that will never match with the one that is possessed by the genuine P2P clients and hence resist any types of payload insertion in P2P network.

5.3 METHODOLOGY OF PRESENTED FRAMEWORK

The proposed system is designed on 32 bit Window 7 OS with minimum 4 GB RAM size. As the experiment is performed on extremely high definition (HD) video of 1080 pixel of MP4 format, so a high speed processor like Intel core i3 is mandatory. The experiment is performed between any numbers of peers; hence the simulation is designed with peer who wants to encrypt the frame that is requested by another peer. The proposed system doesn't use any conventional secret key but uses much advanced version of security using SHA algorithm. The next peer needs to follow the reverse process for decrypting the transmitted frame. In the P2P video stream verification scheme, the SHA-1 algorithm is used for crypto-hash tagging with a size of 160 bits. A digital signature scheme is applied to sign the root packet with 1024 bits of signature overhead. The parameters of network communications are listed as follows. The symbol rate is 1000 kHz and the default channel state factor is -120 dB. The MAC layer fragmentation overhead is six bytes and the acknowledgement overhead is eight bytes. The sleep-wake up interval is 0.1 s. Control packets are transmitted at 20 mW and the receive power is 15 mW. The experiment is performed considering that only after performing encryption, an attacker will attempt to introduce malicious payload into P2P network where an attacker might be protecting themselves using IP spoofing.

The input frames are colored with different dimension and size that were captured using video processing tools in Matlab. All the frames have same dimension, but due to high definition colored frames, the sizes differs in small bits sometimes which is quite normal. The preliminary step will be to be to convert the high definition frames into grayscale. It is very important step for converting as high definition images are quite bigger in size, difficult to compress, difficult to transmit, and highly time consuming in communication, that is ideal situation for initiation attack. Before performing any further processing, the total number of layers as well as payload per layers needs to be ascertained by the peer-1. The application will also be provided with compression ratio of 30:1, 35:1, and 40:1. Now, the considered frame is ready to be performed for encryption procedure. The encryption process starts with decomposing the processed input frame in multi-dimensional levels using discrete wavelet transform. Currently, level 1–8 is formulated. Following are the results after performing decomposition.

The encoding process generated hash links of the payload for which reason even if the attacker introduces any malicious payloads within the frames, the programmers can be easily identified as it will never match with the hash chain used while encryption. This phenomenon will reject even accepting any alien or unknown payload in the network. After the frames are quantized, an entropy coding is applied to the processed payload. This technique makes the payload quite stronger to get encrypted. The next phase will perform video stream verification operation and finally the encryption is performed from peer-1. The encrypted payload is then sent to the network, specifically for entitled peer-2. The payload on the other end has to first get itself authenticated using proposed video stream verification protocol. An entropy decoding is performed followed by dequantization process. Inverse DWT is performed finally to decode the encrypted payload.

Figure 5.2: Frame-1 (Dimension: 1920x812, Size:1.07MB)

Figure 5.3: Frame-2 (Dimension: 1920x812, Size: 1.42MB)

Figure 5.4: Frame-3 (Dimension: 1920x812, Size: 1.15MB)

Figure 5.5: Frame-4 (Dimension: 1920x812, Size: 1.56MB)

The above figure 5.1–5.4 shows the frames that were captured using video processing tools in Matlab. All the frames have same dimension, but due to high definition colored frames, the sizes differs in small bits sometimes which is quite normal. For the purpose of evaluation, we will consider Frame-3 (Figure 5.3) for the further part of protocol implementation using P2P security framework. The preliminary step will be to be to convert the high definition frames into grayscale as shown below:

Figure 5.6: Video frame in Grayscale mode

It is very important step for converting as high definition images are quite bigger in size, difficult to compress, difficult to transmit, and highly time consuming in communication, that is ideal situation for initiation attack. Before performing any further processing, the total number of layers as well as payload per layers needs to be ascertained by the peer-1. The application will also be provided with compression ratio of 30:1, 35:1, and 40:1. Now, the considered frame is ready to be performed for encryption procedure. The encryption process starts with decomposing the processed input frame in multi-dimensional levels using discrete wavelet transform. Currently, level 1–8 is formulated. Following are the results after performing decomposition.

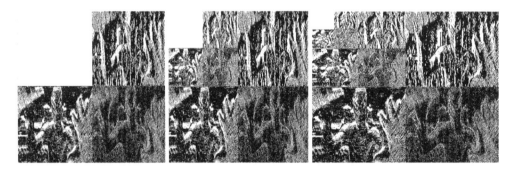

Figure 5.7: Different level decomposition using DWT

Figure 5.8: Video Frame quantization &Dequantization operations

Figure 5.9: Decoded Image

5.4 NUMERICAL ANALYSIS

This section of the book present a numerical analysis by means of presenting a performance evaluation. For the purpose of performance analysis, we select the very recent work done Castro, Alves, and Andrade [12]. The authors have presented an effective solution for reliable commercial P2P content delivery that is claimed to provide necessary support for a real time online business model. The work has considered the case study of P2PTube which is open source software to stream movies on the internet.

The work has drawn the attention as the proposed system is about securing the multimedia content over the P2P network without using conventional cryptography that has complex key management. Hence, it is required to compare the work with [12]. Another work which has drawn the attention is SypeMorph [13] that was designed by Moghaddam and Li. The authors have designed a model in which the peer user obfuscates its messages to the bridge in a widely used protocol over internet.

The best part of the work is their attempt to distinguish between the obfuscated bridge connection and actual Skype video call using statistical comparison. The proposed work that uses SHA-1 as a representation of Crypthash tagging mechanism is yet to be explored for its robustness when it comes to more real time work like [13]. Hence, it is decided to conduct performance analysis based on parameters like Simulation Speed, Quantum of unauthorized peer request, Inter-packet delay, and Bandwidth consumption.

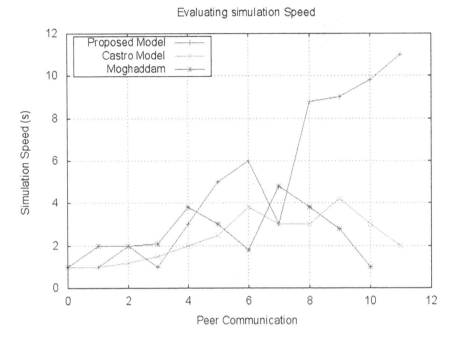

Figure 5.10: Observed Simulation Speed

Table 5.1: Observed Simulation Speed

X	1	2	3	4	5	6	7	8	9	10	11
Proposed	1	2	1	3	5	6	3	8.8	9	9.8	
Castro	1	1.2	1.5	2	2.5	3.8	3	3	4.2	3	2
Moghaddam	2	2	2.1	3.8	3	1.8	4.8	3.8	2.8	1	

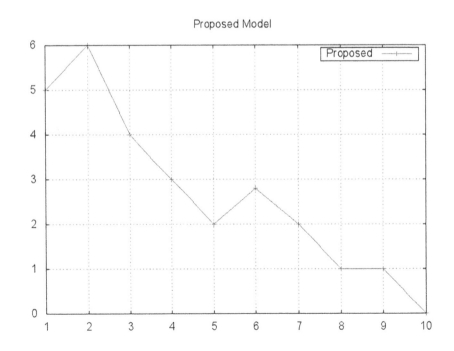

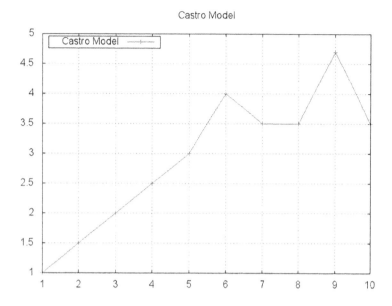

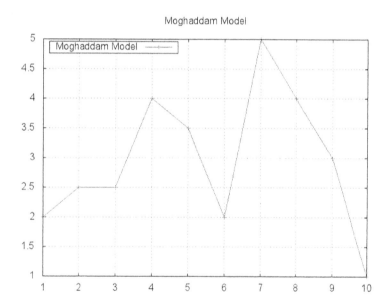

Figure 5.11: Quantum of unauthorized peer request

Table 5.2: Quantum of unauthorized peer request

X	1	2	3	4	5	6	7	8	9	10
Proposed	5	6	4	3	2	2.8	2	1	1	0
Castro	1	1.5	2	2.5	3	4	3.5	3.5	4.7	3.5
Moghaddam	2	2.5	2.5	4	3.5	2	5	4	3	1

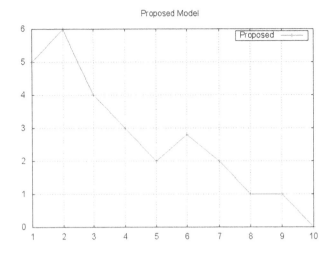

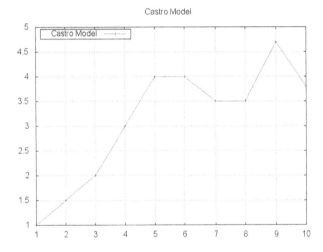

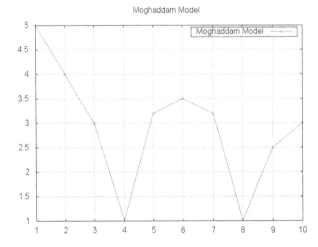

Figure 5.12: Inter-packet delay

Table 5.3: Inter-packet delay

X	1	2	3	4	5	6	7	8	9	10
Proposed	5	6	4	3	2	2.8	2	1	1	0
Castro	1	1.5	2	3	4	4	3.5	3.5	4.7	3.8
Moghaddam	5	4	3	1	3.2	3.5	3.2	1	2.5	3

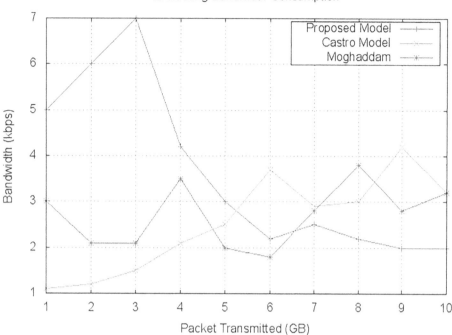

Figure 5.13: Bandwidth Consumption

Table 5.4: Bandwidth Consumption

X	1	2	3	4	5	6	7	8	9	10
Proposed	5	6	7	4.2	3	2.2	2.5	2.2	2	2
Castro	1.1	1.2	1.5	2.1	2.5	3.7	2.9	3	4.2	3.2
Moghaddam	3	2.1	2.1	3.5	2	1.8	2.8	3.8	2.8	3.2

Figure 5.10 show that the proposed model processes much faster simulation in comparison to Castro Model and Moghaddam-model. From the security point of view, the model is experimented for analyzing unauthorized peer request. Because an effective model should identify as well as restrict the entire illegal request. Figure 5.10 shows that although the proposed technique has initially captured maximum of the request, but with the increase of quantity of peers, number of illegal request are identified as well as minimized too. To some extent Moghaddam model also gives equivalent result. The next parameter will be to understand the inter-packet delay. Here also the proposed model as well as Moghaddam model highly minimizes the inter-packet delay to great extent as shown in Figure 5.12. The last parameter in study will be the overall bandwidth consumption (Fig. 5.13). The proposed system can communicate with maximum numbers of peers with less bandwidth (kbps). This was achieved due to compression technique applied even before performing encryption while sending the payload from sender peer to other peer. Hence the proposed system is capable enough to retain robust security against malicious payload insertion.

5.5 CONCLUSION

The presented framework has considered a large number of payloads in the form of frames extracted from multimedia file over P2P network. Majority of the past work has considered conventional cryptography using simple key management that is not so robust or else implemented with complex cryptographic algorithm that increase bandwidth consumption or maximize network overhead. The proposed system has introduced a secure frame compatible video stream authentication protocol with minimized verification dependency overhead that is extremely easy to be integrated with any network payload allocation. The attack scenario of malicious payload insertion is considered. The simulation result shows that the proposed system has enhance the security level to maximum with less bandwidth consumption. The future work will be to create an optimization for the similar encryption technique with more potential and lightweight encryption algorithm on the top of this.

REFERENCES

[1] T.Do, KA. Hua, and M. Tantaoui, "P2VoD: Providing Fault Tolerant Video-on-Demand Streaming in Peer-to-Peer Environment.," in the Proc. of the IEEE ICC, Paris, France, 2004

[2] Y. Liu, X. Hei, C. Liang, and K. W. ROSS. "Insight into pplive: A measurement study of a largescale P2P iptv system" 2006

[3] Duc A. Tran, Kien A. Hua, and Tai T. Do, "ZIGZAG: An Efficient Peer-to-Peer Scheme for Media Streaming.," In Proceedings of IEEE INFOCOM 2003, San Francisco, CA, USA, Vol.30 Mars – 03 Avril 2003

[4] M. Hefeeda, A. Habib, B. Botev, D. Xu, and B. Bhargava, "PROMISE: Peer-to-Peer Media Streaming Using CollectCast.," In Proc. of ACM Multimedia 2003, pages 45--54, Berkeley, CA, Novembre 2003

[5] Schaar.M.V.D, Turaga.D and Wong.R, "Classification-based system for cross-layer optimized wireless video transmission," IEEE Trans. Multimedia, vol. 8, no. 5, pp. 1082–1095, October, 2006

[6] Christopoulos, C. "The JPEG2000 still image coding system: An overview," IEEE Transactions on Consumer Electronics, vol. 46, No. 4, pp. 1103–1127, November 2000

[7] Qiao.D, Choi.S, Jain.A, and Shin.K. "Miser: An optimal low-energy transmission strategy for IEEE 802.11a/h," in Proc. ACM MobiCom, pp. 161–175.September, 2003

[8] Qiao.D and Shin.K, "Energy-efficient airtime allocation in multi-rate multi-power-level wireless LANs," in Proc. ACM QShine, August, 2007

[9] Schurgers, C Aberthorne, O and Srivastava, M "Modulation scaling for energy aware communication systems," in Proc. Low Power Electronics and Design, pp. 96–99, August, 2001

[10] William.S, "Data and Computer Communications," 7th ed. Upper Saddle River, NJ: Prentice-Hall, pp. 85–86, 2000

[11] Schaar.M.V.D and Turaga.D, "Cross-layer packetization and retransmission strategies for delay-sensitive wireless multimedia transmission," IEEE Trans. Multimedia, vol. 9, no. 1, pp. 185–197, January, 2007

[12] Castro.H, Alves.A. P and Andrade.M.T. "Reliable P2P Content Delivery for Alternative Business Models," International Journal of Computer Information Systems and Industrial Management Applications. ISSN 2150-7988 vol 5, pp. 011–029, 2012.

[13] Moghaddam.H.M, Li. B, Derakhshani.M and Goldberg.I, "Skype Morph: Protocol Obfuscation for Tor Bridges," ACM, 2012

CHAPTER 6

FRAMEWORK FOR EVOLUTIONARY TECHNIQUE FOR P2P SECURITY

6.1 OVERVIEW

This chapter introduces an outline that performs a unique way of encryption on the frames of the multimedia files in P2P network using evolutionary algorithm. The framework ensures that even if the multimedia file is being compromised by any attacker, the file will not be able to be decrypted. Interesting aspect of the frame work is the encryption mechanism of formulated without using conventional and sophisticated cryptographic approach.

The area of modern communication system using Peer-to-Peer (P2P) network is currently adopted by many user for the multimedia sharing purpose. The evolution to streaming and multicast (e.g., TV) was just a consequence. The P2P (Peer-to-Peer) technology is now well-known by the public, mainly because of the great success of some applications, such as file sharing applications (Kazaa, eDonkey, BitTorrent, etc.) but also more recently such as video streaming applications (PPLive, PPStream, UUSee, SopCast, etc.). However, the P2P networks still suffer from bad reputation because of the large number of illegal contents that are distributed by those applications.

The usage of the social networking applications e.g. (Facebook and MySpace) are also on rise as the user find broader set of tools to perform highly customized communication as well as it also enable the user to share their personal data over the internet. Such application has also higher versions of accessibility from various computing devices. Usually social networking applications are client (browser) specific application that permits the user to share their multimedia (image and video) data as well as it also allows the other end of recipient to perform downloading too.

Usage of such application also involves cost of maintenance from server viewpoint. Therefore, a peer-to-peer based technique is the best alternative solution to overcome such load of networking and thereby minimizes cost of maintenance too. But, as peer-to-peer architecture is basically overlay architecture on top of internet protocols, thereby the communication usually takes place directly from one peer to another peer in absence of any intermediate server. Due to the design of peer-to-peer system, it poses potential threats from security viewpoint in terms of secure communication and accessing confidential data.

Such types of application using peer-to-peer networking system are usually shared on public network where the vulnerability of transmitted data (especially over wireless network) poses a potential threat to confidentiality, privacy, as well as integrity as shown in Fig. 1. Excavating the history will highlight multiple formats of attacks in the work of Information Technology [1] introduced by P2P network. The popular product of P2P i.e. Napster has already witnessed such intrusions. Hence, there is a critical need of more investigation towards system designarea in order to furnish a better security protocols for preventing unauthorized intrusions or attacks in such P2P networks.

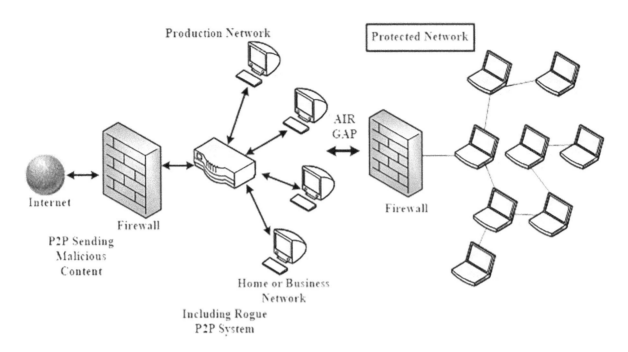

Figure 6.1: Vulnerabilities of P2P network

Due to absence of web or application server to monitor the communication systems in P2P, it basically allows the intruders to formulate various versions of attacks e.g. break-in attack, malicious mischief, espionage etc to name a few. Usage of P2P network allows the user to download various applications that may be pirated or malicious in nature completely harming the entire traffic system routing towards the user and its connected network peripherals too. Hence, security policies are highly vulnerable and susceptible for network breach in P2P applications [2]. Not only security aspect, consistent usage of P2P networks like BitTorrent, Kazaa, etc renders the network completely slow due to high bandwidth consumption. Such issues also give rise to Quality of Service (QoS) problems over internet usage. Unfortunately, the existing P2P networking system resists the corporate network security by furnishing decentralized security administration, decentralized shared data storage system, and a method to prevent critical perimeter defenses e.g. Firewalls, AntiRootKits etc.

In the designed method, the recurrence relation of degree 2 and a key extracted from the multimedia contents are used to encrypt the image. The discussed technique is used to generate a number of encrypted digital contents that are almost near to impossible to decrypt by intruder. These encrypted multimedia contents are considered as the initial population for the evolutionary algorithm which is considered for deployment in the study for the purpose of optimizing the encryption to higher degree. In the end, the best cipher-frame is chosen as the final encryption frame.

The design work carried out attempted to explore some prior work done towards securing image or video contents over P2P network and examined some attacks and issues with P2P networks. In the multimedia content distribution scenario, this server is usually hosted and maintained by the content providers. This results in peer user's anonymity interference and content provider's efforts in server maintenance. It was found that majority of the work done past is either on cryptography or using DRM or watermarking, where the prime concern is the privacy and anonymity issues of content consumers.

Since DRM systems track user transactions, purchases, and access history, end consumers' detail activities are recorded at content retailer's database and thus raise divergences regarding multimedia content protection versus privacy protection. Due to the inherent characteristics of decentralization, P2P network suffers from security loopholes as there is no central monitoring or control system to mitigate the online threats or attacks. No much work towards securing image or video content while transmission is explored very recently or even in past.

6.2 ANALYTICAL DESIGN AND SYSTEMATIC MODELLING

The systematic model leads a novel computational method of secure multimedia transmission in P2P set-up. The system uses the potentials of recurrence relation of degree 2. Recurrence relation [3] were applied in various fields in past as it basically defines recursively a sequence once one or more initial terms are given where each further term of the sequence is defined as a function of the preceding terms. The relation of is represented as:

$$x_{n+1} = rx_n(1-x_n) \hspace{4cm} (6.1)$$

Where, x_n is a number with a range of 0–1 and it signifies the ratio of current population to the highest potential population at year n, r is a positive number that represents a combined rate for reproduction and starvation. Equation (6.1) shows a nonlinear difference equation that is intended to encapsulate two impacts e.g. a) reproduction where the population will increase at a rate proportional to the current population when the population size is small and b) starvation (density-dependent mortality) where the growth rate will decrease at a rate proportional to the value obtained by taking the theoretical "carrying capacity" of the environment less the current population.

Recurrence relation is applied over the encryption process to generate certain initial values that will be used further for optimization of encryption processes. As the optimization technique will require a population (scores of best encryption), hence, recurrence relation formulation assists in generation those initial values that will be a part of computation for best population selection (strongest encryption over the multimedia contents) using a fitness function.

The analytical model uses recurrence relation of degree 2 and a key extracted from the extracted multimedia contents are used to encrypt the file. The design scheme using recurrence relation is used to generate quantity of the population (encrypted digital of multimedia files to be transmitted). These encrypted digital contents are considered as the initial population for the evolutionary algorithm. Then, the evolutionary algorithm is used to optimize the encryption process as much as possible. At the end, the optimal ciphered multimedia content is selected as the final encryption content. The book also discusses the techniques deployed in use of recurrence relation and evolutionary algorithms and consecutively, the accomplished results were analyzed with concluding remarks. Therefore, this book chapter target of the design system is to formulate a secure, efficient, and computationally less expensive process that ensures safer protection of multimedia contents. In order to accomplish the chapter target, following objectives needs to be considered:

> To design 2 modules to implement the analytical scheme e.g. Peer-1 for performing encryption and peer 2 for performing decryption module.
> To design a framework for accepting the input frames and perform portioning to 4 equal parts based on the specified dimension of the frames.
> To implement recurrence relation of degree 2 by selecting specific pixels as encryption key for forming the initial value and for performing encryption towards the input frames.
> To estimate the initial value of the recurrence relation.
> To strengthen the encryption technique using secret key.
> To optimize the encryption method using Evolutionary algorithm.
> To restore and access the encrypted frames for performing decryption operation by peer-2 client.
> To perform the entire operation considering image entropy, correlation coefficient, and key analysis.

6.3 DESIGN METHODOLOGY

In this part of the chapter discusses the system design methodology. The system design firstassumes a highly vulnerable P2P connectivity on either wired network or in wireless network. However, the current work only emphasizes on the security aspect of the multimedia contents to be transmitted by Peer-1 to Peer-N. The current work considers a frame as an input towards the framework which it partitions in 4 equal quadrants based on the cumulative dimension of input frame (Table 6.1). To make the computation easier, the colored frames are converted to grayscale that is subjected to the actual algorithm. The design scheme considers using recurrence relation for performing encryption on all the pixels presents in each of the 4 partitioned image blocks. The design scheme considers the input of video file of MP4 format of size 268 KB as shown below in Figure 6.2, which is finally converted to grayscale for ease in computation.

Figure 6.2: Extracted frames for the input to the model

Step-1: The system considers 5 pixel selections from each parts of image as the encryption key for designing the initial value of recurrence relation of degree 2 and for performing encryption on that partitioned part. The selections of such pixels are based on the quantity of the population being formed.

Step-2: The preliminary value of the recurrence relation of degree 2 is evaluated from the following equation by using the values of the gray scales of the five pixels in step-1.

$$P_x = \{P \times 1, P \times 2, P \times 3, P \times 4, P \times 5\}(in\ decimal) \tag{6.2}$$

Where Pi represents an 8-bit block, then the following equation is used to convert Px into ASCII number.

$$B = \{P1,1, P1,2, P1,3....P2,1, P2,2...P5,7, P5,8\}(in ASCII)$$

Here, Pi,j represents jth bit of the ith block. After Px is converted into an ASCII number, the string B with length of 40 bits is generated. Therefore, by using the following equation, the preliminary values for starting the execution of the recurrence relation of degree 2 is extracted,

$$U_{o,k} = \frac{P_{1,1}x2^{39} + P_{1,2}x2^{38} + ... + P_{2,1}x2^{31} + ... + P_{5,7}x2^1 + P_{5,8}x2^0}{2^{40}} \tag{6.3}$$

Where, k is set of integers for the purpose of indexing each multimedia packet to be used in encryption process. By deploying this relation, the preliminary value of the recurrence function (Uo,k), which lies in the interval 0 to 1 is obtained.

Step-3: The previous step is iterated for each part of the plain frames. Hence, at the end, there will be 4 distinct preliminary values for each portioned portion of the frames.

Step-4: For encryption the pixels in each part of the image, the preliminary value of that part and following equation is deployed,

$$CurrentValue = round(U_{i,k} x255) \otimes OldValue \qquad (6.4)$$

In the above equation, XOR operation is performed, and OldValue represents the existing value of the pixel and CurrentValue represents the new value of the pixel after it is encrypted. The value of $U_{i,k}$ refers to the ith value of the recurrence relation in the kth part of the original frame that is determined for each step by using equation (6.1).

All the pixels in each part, except the 5 pixels used as the key, are sequentially (row by row) encrypted in this way. Finally, the first member of the population is built. These steps are repeated for the entire partitioned image to get the rest of the population.

6.4 PERFORMANCE EVALUATION AND OUTCOME

This section discusses the performance analysis of the system design. With the application of a multimedia encryption algorithm to any multimedia contents, its pixels values change when compared with the original frames. The deign framework was project to make such alterations in pixel values in extremely irregular and sophisticated fashion for maximizing the higher degree of pixel differences between the original and encrypted multimedia contents.

The core of the technique considers the higher flexibility in encryption by creating maximum random patterns that have no chance of disclosing any private characteristics of the original multimedia contents. However, it should be noted that there should not be any sorts of dependent between the encrypted and original multimedia contents. The encoded multimedia content should have very low value of correlation compared to original multimedia content. Another critical factor in evaluating an encrypted multimedia content is the visual inspection process.

The design method has also considered diffusion as one of the significant factor for measuring the randomization of the encryption process. It is strongly believed that if the presented algorithm has better diffusion features than the correlation between the original and encrypted multimedia contents will be very much complex and thereby highly unpredictable.

Table 6.1: Outcome of Simulation

Block	Encryption	Block	Decryption
Input		input	

Block	Encryption	Block	Decryption

In order to scale up the diffusion characteristics of the system design, a bit of pixel is changed in source content and the error estimation between the encrypted multimedia contents accomplished from original source content were evaluated. The parameters for evaluation of the P2P network security process are discussed below:-

> **Estimating Entropy for Frames**:-Entropy is one of the prominent features in randomization and is basically a mathematical modeling for data communication and storage systems. Equation 6.1 is introduced for obtaining entropy.

$$H(S) = \sum_{i=0}^{2^N-1} P(s_i)\log(\frac{1}{P(s_i)}) \tag{6.5}$$

Where N is the number of gray levels used in the multimedia contents, and $P(s_i)$ illustrates the probability of having a ith gray level in the multimedia contents. In multimedia contents that are generated in a completely random way, the presented formulation considers N as 8 to be an ideal value.

> **Pearson Product-Moment Correlation Coefficient**:-A good encryption algorithm is one in which the correlation coefficient between pairs of encrypted adjacent pixels in the horizontal, vertical, and diagonal positions are at the least possible level. The correlation coefficient is calculated by using equation 6.5

$$r_{xy} = \frac{|\operatorname{cov}(x,y)|}{\sqrt{D(x)}x\sqrt{D(y)}} \tag{6.6}$$

In the above relation, x and y are the gray levels in two adjacent pixels of the frames. In calculating the correlation coefficients, the following equations are employed:

$$\text{cov}(x, y) = \frac{1}{N} \sum_{i=1}^{N} (x_i - E(x)) (y_i - E(y)) \tag{6.7}$$

$$E(x) = \frac{1}{N} \sum_{i=1}^{N} x_i$$

$$D(x) = \frac{1}{N} \sum_{i=1}^{N} (x_i - E(x))^2$$

To test the correlation coefficient between two adjacent vertical pixels, two adjacent horizontal pixels, and two adjacent diagonal pixels in a cipher-frame, the following procedure is used: first, 2500 pairs of pixels are randomly selected, and then the correlation coefficient is obtained by using equation5 (the results of which are shown in Table 6.2).

Table 6.2: PPMCC of two adjacent pixels in two images

	Plain-Frame	Cipher-Frame
Vertical	0.9711	0.0093
Horizontal	0.9445	-0.0054
Diagonal	0.9217	-0.0009

➢ **Key analysis**: A suitable encryption algorithm must be sensitive to small changes in keys. Moreover, the key must be long enough to resist against brute-force attacks. In the design, a 40-bit long key is suggested which produces a key space equivalent to 240 (and hence this key seems to be long enough). To test the sensitivity of the key in the model, first the frame is encrypted using the design techniques. Then, this same frame is encrypted once again using the design technique, with the difference that this time, in the stage of producing the initial population (when each member of the population is being produced), one bit of the key of the member is changed; and the population is formed in this way. After this new population is formed, the rest of the exhibited method is executed, and in the end final frame is obtained. The experiment also shows the similarity of the two encrypted images (the white points are the common points of the two encrypted frames). The two encrypted frames are about 99.76% different.

After forming the initial population, the evolutionary algorithm is used to optimize the encrypted images. The evolutionary algorithm introduced in the scheme that uses the multi-point crossover operation. The design scheme is experimented on 32 bit Windows OS with 2.84 GHz Intel core i3 processor considering Matlab as the programming tool. The design system considers frames (still image) and converts it in grayscale in case the origin image is colored as shown in Figure 6.3(a). The input frame is then partitioned into 4 equal quadrants (portions) as seen in Figure 6.3(b). The preliminary values are estimated exactly after that along with implementation of recurrent relation and secret key which is user defined.

Figure 6.3: (a). Input (b) Partitioning into 4 equal quadrants

Figure 6.4: Process of performing encryption in each partitioned frames portion

Finally a decryption mechanism is performed considering the encrypted image as input image along with previously used secret key. Following are the results accomplished.

Figure 6.5: Input encrypted image

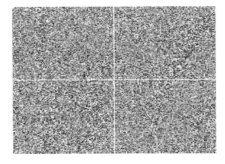

Figure 6.6: Partitioning into 4 equal quadrants

Figure 6.7: Process of performing decryption in each partitioned (encrypted frames)

Baboon

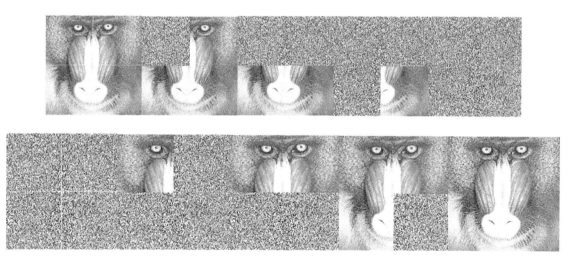

Barbara

Cameraman

Figure 6.8: Evaluation with other standard dataset

The system design is also evaluated with other standard dataset as exhibited in Fig. 6.8. The exhibited system considers correlation coefficient between the pairs of adjacent pixel value of each frames extracted from video as the fitness function. At each stage, the new generations produced and the previous ones are evaluated using the fitness function and 50% of the population with the minimum PPM-correlation coefficient and 10% of the remaining population is selected for the next generations. In every generation, the initial values and correlation values that are considered as encryption parameters are checked during optimization internally by the evolutionary algorithm. This is an iterative process until it finds the best correlation coefficient as the best generation when it doesn't show much significant change in dual successive stages of iterations. Followed by the previous step, the generation with minimum correlation value is finally considered for encryption.

For the purpose of comparative analysis, the system design is compared with the study done by Tedmori and Najdawi [4]. The prime reason behind it is that the design scheme performs encryption without using cryptographic approach, where it is essential to understand how the analytical scheme furnishes better security strength as compared to frequently adopted cryptographic techniques for securing images.

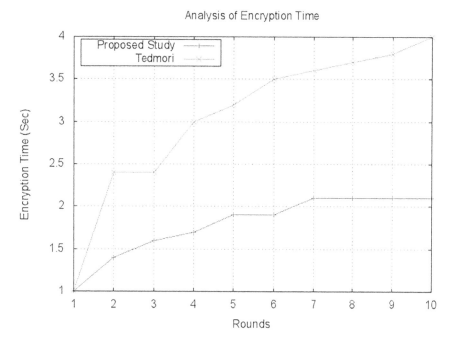

Figure 6.9: Analysis of Encryption Time

Table 6.3: Analysis of Encryption Time

X	1	2	3	4	5	6	7	8	9	10
Proposed	1	1.4	1.6	1.7	1.9	1.9	2.1	2.1	2.1	2.1
Tedmori	1	2.4	2.4	3	3.2	3.5	3.6	3.7	3.8	4

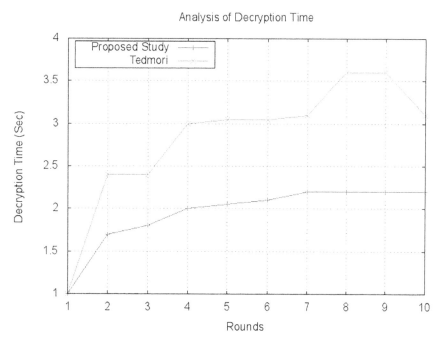

Figure 6.10: Analysis of Decryption Time

Table 6.4: Analysis of Decryption Time

X	1	2	3	4	5	6	7	8	9	10
Proposed	1	1.7	1.8	2	2.05	2.1	2.2	2.2	2.2	2.2
Tedmori	1	2.4	2.4	3	3.05	3.05	3.1	3.6	3.6	3.1

Fig. 6.9 and Fig. 6.10 highlights the encryption and decryption time in seconds for the design system as well as Tedmori approach [4]. Tedmori approach initially transforms image into frequency domain, where the author have used DCT technique to convert the target image into frequency domain and thereby perform encryption. The system has an obvisous complexity in encryption as while the input from preprocessed 8 x 8 blocks are integer-valued, the output values are typically real-valued. Thus we need a quantization step to make some decisions about the values in each DCT block and produce output that is interger-valued. Hence, encryption time for Tedmori approach is found quite higher with in the increasing rounds (increasing number of images in each consecutive round) as compared to demonstrated system.

6.5 CONCLUSION

The P2P network design highlights a new method for performing encryption over the multimedia contents by using recurrence relation of degree 2 and evolutionary algorithm. The system uses recurrence relation for the preliminary encryption and the evolutionary algorithm is deployed to strength then encryption process in P2P network further more secure. The accomplished results from correlation coefficients and the entropies of the images also prove the high efficiency of presented method.

REFERENCES

[1] F. Pianese, J. Keller, and E. W. Biersack, "PULSE, a Flexible P2P Live Streaming System," in Proc. of 9th IEEE Global Internet Symposium Barcelona, Spain, 28 & 29 April 2006

[2] Nicolas Christin, Andreas S. Weigend and John Chuang, Content Availability, "Pollution and Poisoning in Peer-to-Peer File Sharing Networks," Proceedings of the 6th ACM conference on Electronic commerce, 2005

[3] "Recurrence relation," http://en.wikipedia.org/wiki/Recurrence_relation, Retrieved on 14 June, 2018

[4] S. Tedmori and N.A-Najdawi, "Lossless Image Cryptography Algorithm Based on Discrete Cosine Transform," the Internal Arab Journal of Information Technology, Vol. 9, No. 5, 2012

CHAPTER 7

CORE FINDING OF THE STUDY

7.1 OVERVIEW

In this chapter the system design of the presented scheme is concluding that the Peer to Peer network is one of the frequently used applications in terms of file sharing over a global large network. In such types of network, there can exist an illegitimate peer node who will attempt to have an unauthorized access to premium digital content. As it is very difficult to catch hold of the intruder or the illegal client inside the network, the proposed system will at least attempt to prevent access to the digital content available. The demonstrated scheme is focused on multimedia file sharing where the protocol will be designed in such a way that whenever any unauthorized peer node will attempt to download any premium digital content, the proposed model will assign a poison chunk of data to be forwarded to the illegitimate client. This phenomenon will result in exponential increase of download time rending discouragement to download the same file by the illegal downloader. While the protocol assures the secure delivery of the cleaner chunk of data to the legitimate client.

The design scheme discusses about a unique approach for facilitating security towards the multimedia contents in Peer-to-Peer (P2P) network like Gnutella and Kazaa. The last decade has seen a huge range of research interest towards multimedia distribution along with delivery of live streaming of digital media. One of the major concern with the existing system is that there is enough security against the digital contents in P2P network which renders the service provider little hesitant to deploy the service towards its paid client. Till now, there is no such technology or software application which ensures the secure delivery of genuine digital multimedia content toward its client's end. Another issue in adoption of this technology is the messy organization of overlay network which lead to network overhead thereby indirectly consumes the bandwidth and other network resources unwontedly. The presented method, highlight about a novel approach of implementing a security framework in P2P network which ensures a secure and authenticated delivery of genuine and legitimate contents to its paid clients. Simulation results shows that deployment of presented algorithm provides sufficient security to the communication channel and also ensures the proper delivery of the multimedia contents

The analytical design introduces a novel technique of mitigating malicious payload insertion in P2P network by designing a robust Video Streaming Verification Protocol (VSVP) considering advanced encryption technique on individual frames of the video. Considering increasing challenging situation, a high definition (HD) video of MP4 format is selected and VSVP is implemented over individual frames of the video. The encryption scheme towards the payload is performed using DWT and an efficient compression ratio is considered for minimizing the bandwidth consumption. The resolution and frames distortion is estimated alongside from SNR and BPP. The system can be evaluated with multiple layers of payload as well as payload for each layer. The whole system is evaluated with unequally protected payloads also with the assumption of VSVP. The simulation shows an efficient result with high potential to resist malicious payload insertion.

Distribution and sharing of multimedia contents is extensively higher in number as compared to other applications in Peer-to-Peer network. The prior work in the same issues is conducted to explore that there are comparatively few work done when it comes to ensuring security over transmitting multimedia contents over highly vulnerable P2P network. Therefore, this book introduces a cost-effective and trivial model using recurrence relation of degree 2 and evolutionary algorithm for performing multimedia content encryption. A novel technique of performing encryption using a simple partitioning technique is used to ensure the security of the transmitted frames over any types of network. The novelty of the exhibited scheme is that evolutionary algorithm is used for strengthening the encryption process further and final results were evaluated with respect to maximized entropy of frames, minimized Pearson Product Moment Correlation Coefficient (PPMCC) among the adjacent pixels and key analysis.

The main objective of the book is to evolve a framework for security in order to achieve overall architectural model. In objective one the traditional poisoning method is enhanced and robustness parameters considered are download time is found to be uniform even after varying the data size and processing time is found to be lesser than existing approaches considered. In objective two is a novel mechanism for secure routing is explored and robustness parameters considered are compression of multimedia file, time to detect watermarking, Packet delivery ratio, Video quality for peers with different download bandwidths, processing time and packet delay reduction. In objective three Payload insertion mechanism is proposed from the viewpoint of data integrity and robustness parameters considered are quantum of unauthorized peer request which was found almost zero, inter packet delay limiting to null and bandwidth consumption was lower than existing techniques considered and finally, in objective four an optimized model for security is established and robustness parameters considered are encryption and decryption time, which were observed to be lower than existing techniques considered.

7.2 SCOPE/LIMITATION

The scope/limitations of the current study are as follows:

➢ The current study on security of multimedia transmission has been mainly considered using the case study of BitTorrent, Gnutella, and Kazaa. Hence, all the analysis results concretely provide substantial evidence of effective security in this consideration of P2P multimedia security. However, as the approach of the study is completely mathematical and simulation based, so, the outcome of the study needs more analysis towards its compatibility / supportability in other P2P protocols like WinMX, eDonkey, BearShare, and Morpheus.

➢ The current study has mainly considered only JPEG / Bitmapped format image and MPEG format videos to carry out the experiments as these are the frequently used multimedia format in P2P network.

➢ The current study has adopted mainly genetic algorithm as evolutionary technique where if the population size is too small, the genetic algorithm may not explore enough of the solution space to consistently find good solutions. If the rate of genetic change is too high or the selection scheme is chosen poorly, beneficial schema may be disrupted and the population may enter error catastrophe, changing too fast for selection to ever bring about convergence. However, by accomplishing anticipated results, research objective is achieved.

➢ The adversarial model considered for current study is malicious payload insertion which is quite novel attacking concept never explored before. However, it is out of scope of the book to explain how far effective the current mitigation technique is in mitigating other adversaries too in P2P network.

7.3 CONTRIBUTORY ASPECTS

The contributions of the current study are as follows:-

1. The first significant contribution of the current study is to introduce a hybrid framework for mitigating illegitimate peer nodes in multimedia file sharing in P2P network. The study has successfully accomplished following operation that predominantly mitigate any sorts of unauthorized peer request e.g. i) Error-free identification of colluders and pirates, ii) Creation of secure protocol for forwarding poisoned chunk of data to illegitimate client in network, and iii) Creation of protocol for preventing colluders to come in contact with legitimate clients in the network. The study has effectively stopped collusive piracy within the boundary of a P2P content delivery network. The protection scheme works nicely in a P2P network environment.

2. The second significant contribution of the current study is to design a framework for secure routing for shielding the multimedia contents in P2P network. This phase of the study has successfully accomplished following security parameters e.g. i) authenticating users, in order to allow only authorized people to join the system, ii) verifying the identity of passing content to allow only authorized content to be exchange, iii) analyzing the flows exchanged between the various entities in the system (including peers) to detect malicious behaviors that may attack the system or alter its efficiency.

3. The third significant contribution of the current study is to present a framework for resisting malicious payload insertion for securing video streaming over P2P network. The study uses JPEG2000 encoding and decoding schema as here the decoding of each high definition (HD) layer packets depends on successful decoding of those packets in the same code block or sectors from previous quality layer. Hence, it is felt that it is highly reasonable to match the crypto-hash link dependency assignment during the authentication process to the image decoding dependency. Since, the crypto-hash tag of the HD layers is attached to previous layers packet, the authentication rate-distortion performance can be highly optimized. Therefore, it can be said that unification between image payload authentication in P2P network and its decoding is highly challenging task. The framework essentially quantifies the relationship between two factors, i.e. i) the P2P network resource allocation and ii) the frames distortion during transmission

4. The fourth contribution of the current study is to introduce a framework for secure multimedia transmission in P2P using recurrence relation and evolutionary algorithm. The study has successfully accomplished the better security optimization by following operations e.g. i) designing 2 modules to implement the proposed system e.g. a) Peer-1 for performing encryption and b) Peer-2 for performing decryption module, ii) designing a framework for accepting the input frames and perform portioning to 4 equal parts based on the specified dimension of the frames, and iii) implementing recurrence relation of degree 2 by selecting specific pixels as encryption key for forming the initial value and for performing encryption towards the input frames, iv) Estimate the initial value of the recurrence relation, iv) Strengthening the encryption technique using secret key, v) Optimizing the encryption method using Evolutionary algorithm, vi) Restoring and access the encrypted frames for performing decryption operation by peer-2 client, and vii) Performing the entire operation considering image entropy, correlation coefficient, and key analysis.

7.4 FURTHER STUDY

This version of the book has formulated a possible scenario where the inflictions of the attacker or any types of illegitimate peers are possibly high. However, the existing framework could be enhanced by incorporating further cryptographic measures along with swarm intelligence. Different evolutionary and intelligence algorithms can be conceptualized. The existing study covers the multimedia file as image and video files, hence, further study could be done considering audio/speech file.